Battlegrou
NORM.

GW00384064

OPERATION
EPSOM

NORMANDY, JUNE 1944

With the continued expansion of the Battleground series a **Battleground Series Club** has been formed to benefit the reader. The purpose of the Club is to keep members informed of new titles and to offer many other reader-benefits. Membership is free and by registering an interest you can help us predict print runs and thus assist us in maintaining the quality and prices at their present levels.

Please call the office 01226 734555, or send your name and address along with a request for more information to:

Battleground Series Club Pen & Sword Books Ltd,
47 Church Street, Barnsley, South Yorkshire S70 2AS

Cover art is ***Counter Attack at Villers Bocage*** by David Pentland/Cranston Fine Arts.
www.davidpentland.com

Battleground Europe
NORMANDY

OPERATION EPSOM

NORMANDY, JUNE 1944

Tim Saunders

LEO COOPER

This book is dedicated with love to my wife Kate, whose patience, support and understanding is both essential and greatly appreciated.

OTHER BOOKS IN THE SERIES BY TIM SAUNDERS
Hill 112 – Normandy
Hell's Highway – Market Garden
The Island – Market Garden
Nijmegen – Market Garden
Gold Beach-JIG – Normandy

Published by
LEO COOPER
an imprint of
Pen & Sword Books Limited
47 Church Street, Barnsley, South Yorkshire S70 2AS
Copyright © Tim Saunders, 2003

ISBN 0 85052 954 9

A CIP catalogue of this book is available
from the British Library

Printed by CPI UK

*For up-to-date information on other titles produced under the Leo Cooper
imprint, please telephone or write to:*
Pen & Sword Books Ltd, FREEPOST, 47 Church Street
Barnsley, South Yorkshire S70 2AS
Telephone 01226 734222

CONTENTS

11th Armoured Division (159 Brigade) Infantrymen advancing to close with the enemy.

ACKNOWLEDGEMENTS

As is the case with every author of Second World War military history, I am indebted to those on both German side and British veterans who wrote or have been prepared to give me accounts of the battles in which they fought. Publishers and authors have been most generous in allowing me to quote from their work. Also, deserving grateful thanks are those who work in the institutions that care for and make available historical records and books to authors. Chief amongst these are the Public Record Office, the Imperial War Museum and military libraries, such as the peerless Prince Consorts in Aldershot. Regimental museums and regimental headquarters have also patiently trawled their archives for obscure details at my request. I thank them for their help and kindness. However, above all, it is the unique veterans' contributions that makes the Battleground series a success.

I would also like to thank Roni Wilkinson, Chief Designer of the Battleground series, for his patient advice and all that he does to quietly ensure that I keep within my brief. His work in bringing pictures and maps together with the text, to enhance the value of an author's work never ceases to amaze me. I would also like to acknowledge the part played by the other helpful, friendly and supportive staff at Pen and Sword's offices in Barnsley. To those students of military history who are tempted to pick up the pen and write, I say, 'share your ideas, as it will be an enjoyable and rewarding experience'.

In common with most authors of military history, I have to juggle full time employment, family and writing. Therefore, I am indebted to my wife Kate, to whom I have dedicated this book, for her tolerance, support and encouragement over the years.

A Scottish infantry patrol lie up as enemy move across their front.

INTRODUCTION

'You will enter the Continent of Europe and, in conjunction with the other Allied Nations, undertake operations aimed at the heart of Germany and the destruction of her Armed Forces. ...exploitation will be directed towards securing an area that will facilitate both ground and air operations against the enemy.'

Combined Chiefs of Staff's instruction to General Eisenhower.

In contemplating COSSAC's instructions above, General Eisenhower's mission analysis would have focused his attention on seizing a sizeable lodgement in Normandy to accommodate the infrastructure of the armies and airforces. By mid June, General Montgomery who, under Eisenhower, had mapped out progress to accommodate the competing demands of the three Services, had been unable to secure as much territory as planned. On D-Day the troops had expended their energy on breaking into Continental Europe and particularly on the eastern flank, around Caen, failed to reach their objectives. During the following week the German reaction to the invasion had been swift and the Allied drive inland less emphatic than had been expected. Consequently, the Allies were contained in a tight beachhead that lacked both operational depth and real estate.

Within a week of D-Day the invasion euphoria was beginning to wear off and both the generals and air marshals in the UK were beginning to criticise Montgomery. By the end of the second week, an element of the press was becoming critical of the slow progress as the German panzer divisions 'roped off' the Allied lodgement. Montgomery was already under pressure to deliver Caen, space for airfields and 'a breakout' to the press corps. Operation EPSOM, delayed by the storm of 19 – 22 June, was to be Montgomery's answer to his critics.

This book concentrates on the main axis of Operation EPSOM and the battles fought on it by 15th Scottish and 11th Armoured Divisions between 26 June and 30 June 1944. This covers the official EPSOM period up to and including II SS *Panzerkorps'* initial counter-attack. Space precludes fully covering 49th West Riding Division's attack on the Rauray Spur (Operation MARTLET). This operation on the western flank is covered in outline to reflect its role in Montgomery's overall design for battle. I hope that the battle for Rauray will, in due course, become a *Battleground* title in it own right.

There are several other points that I would like to explain at this juncture. The first is, as is customary practice in the *Battleground* series, I have used the correct form of SS ranks rather than English translations or *Wehrmacht* ranks. Therefore, I have included a table at the back of the book (Appendix C) listing equivalent SS, British and American ranks. Secondly, I wish to alert readers to the potential for confusion between SS-*Standartenführer* Kurt

Meyer, nicknamed 'Panzermeyer', the commander of the *Hitlerjugend* and his Chief of Staff SS-*Sturmbannführer* Hubert Meyer. Both of these offices, as key figures, are extensively quoted in this book. Thirdly, in most cases I have let the word 'sniper' stand in the text, although very few of the 'snipers' referred to in quotes were little more than determined 'isolated riflemen' taking shots at opportunity targets. Finally, it would also become tedious to repeatedly point out that the vast majority of German 'Tiger' tank sightings, observations and claims of kills were the result of what commanders refered to as 'Tiger phobia'. In fact, most encounters with enemy armour were either with the most numerous Mark IVs or Panthers and that no more than ten Tigers were operational at any one time on the EPSOM/ MARTLET front.

At home or on the ground, enjoy the tour. *TJJS* WARMINSTER

Above: Mk V Panther.

Above right: British troops moving up during Operation Epsom.

Right: A 105mm Wespe of the type used in the self-propelled artillery batteries in SS Panzer Divisions.

The storm of 19-22 June destroyed the American Mulberry Harbour and badly damaged the British port at Arromanches, seriously delaying the Allied build up.

OMAHA Beach with a newly constructed airfield. Airfields were urgently required by the Allies for use by fighter bombers.

CHAPTER ONE

Background

In his 'Presentation of the Plans', at St Paul's School, London, on 7 April 1944, General Montgomery displayed a series of lines on a map of Normandy, showing 21st Army Group's expected progress to the Rivers Seine and the Loire. General Eisenhower, flanked by his senior naval, land and air planning officers, listened to Montgomery's outline of OVERLORD. Explaining the revised version of COSSAC's plan, Montgomery told them that he had increased both the frontage of the invasion and the number of the airborne and amphibious assault divisions to be committed on D-Day. Montgomery recounted:

> 'It was vital to secure an adequate bridgehead at the outset, so that operations could be developed from a firm and sufficiently spacious base; in any event the area we could hope to seize and hold in the first days of the invasion would become very congested.'

Far more importantly, Montgomery stressed the need to hold the Germans on the Caen front, while the Americans cleared the Cotentin Peninsular and captured the port of Cherbourg. Montgomery analysed the 'run of rail and road communications leading to Normandy', and believed that:

> 'Since the bulk of the enemy mobile reserve was located north of the Seine they would have to approach Normandy from the east and might be expected to converge on Caen.'

In summary, the need for sufficient ground in the beachhead and the need to fight to hold the Germans on the Caen front eventually led to the launch of Operation EPSOM.

Allied Progress Since D-Day

The first phase of the invasion had gone well. By the end of the first week, the beachheads had been linked up and progress inland had been sufficient to regard the Allied

11

Despite the storm delaying the Allied build up, the Germans could not match the Allies because of the air attacks and sabotage to the French transport system. These Tigers of 101st SS Schwere Panzer Battalion are having to drive to the Normandy front.

lodgement as secure. However, the area that Montgomery had intended to 'seize and hold in the first days of the invasion' was in the event much smaller than planned. After initial paralysis, effective German reaction had hemmed the Allies into their beachhead.

In some hard fighting, First US Army, consisting of nine divisions, was making steady progress up the Cotentin Peninsular towards Cherbourg and had almost reached the western coast of the Peninsula. On the British front, 3rd Division's D-Day mission had been to take Caen. This it failed to do and Montgomery was soon under significant pressure to create space for Leigh-Mallory's Second Tactical Airforce's airfields and the Army Group's logistic infrastructure. Nevertheless, with the build-up of Allied ground troops exceeding that of the Germans, Montgomery was able to pursue his overall strategy of fighting the German armour on the Caen front. However, he was forced to recognize the importance of capturing ground around Caen rather than focusing on the defeat of the enemy.

Montgomery's second all out attempt to seize Caen was launched from the west, after some heavy fighting east of the River Orne, on 12 June. 7th Armoured Division attacked into a thinly held gap in the enemy line between Caumont and Villers-Bocage. One officer wrote:

> 'Here we were in this first week of battle exploiting a possible breakthrough with very little opposition, an armoured brigade in front and the infantry coming along behind in lorries. It was exciting to be on the move at such a pace.'

All this, however, ended at 0800 hours on 13 June when the Division, led by the Cromwell tanks of A Squadron 4th County of London Yeomanry, entered Villers-Bocage. Here they fell prey to four Tigers of SS-*Obersturmführer* Michel Wittmann's Number 2 Company, 101 SS *Schwere* Panzer Battalion. The British tanks were 'brewed up' one after the other and the accompanying motor battalion of infantry were machine-gunned before they could respond. 7th Armoured Division was halted in its tracks. The battle lasted all day, costing Britain's most glamorous formation twenty-five armoured vehicles and a considerable proportion of the desert veteran's vaunted reputation. With the stopping of 7th Armoured Division's advance, the Germans had managed to form a solid front, through which, future British or Canadian attacks, would have to fight, before the tanks of the armoured divisions could again be unleashed. However, before such a breakthrough could be contemplated, Second Army would have to gather its

Right: SS-Obersturmführer Michael Wittmann and the results of his action at Villers-Bocage. He also commanded his Kompanie of Tigers from 101 SS Schwere Pz Bn during Operation EPSOM.

strength, as the landing programme was already falling behind the planned rates of build-up.

The German Strategy

Convinced by the Allied deception plan, code named FORTITUDE, Hitler and his staff in Berlin (OKW), still believed that the main Allied landing would strike the Fifteenth *Armee* in the *Pas de Calais*. However, with the failure to 'throw the Allies back into the sea', and with the Allies firmly established ashore, *Panzergruppe* West was demanding the dispatch of powerful panzer formations to counter-attack the lodgement. Six panzer divisions were soon on their way to Normandy from as far afield as Southern France (2nd *Das Reich* SS Panzer Division) and Russia (II SS *Panzerkorps*). The German aim was to mount a powerful counter-stroke against the Allies' centre, driving north to the coast, between First US and Second British Armies and destroying them. The reinforced *Panzergruppe* West would then be available to support Fifteenth *Armee* in defeating a subsequent landing by General Patton's fictitious First US Army Group.

Concentration of the panzer divisions, however, took much longer than expected; such was the effect of Allied bombing, special forces raids on nodal points in the transport network and air interdiction in both France and the Low Countries. Thus the formations that Hitler had released to the Seventh *Armee* in Normandy, were not only badly delayed *en route* but also reduced in combat effectiveness. For example, II SS *Panzerkorps* was forced to de-train in eastern France by Allied air sorties and make a tiring and mechanically wearing road move to Normandy; a distance of four hundred miles. Meanwhile, the panzer formations already in theatre, were committed to holding ground against the British and Canadians, as infantry divisions were also delayed and were making their way, on foot, to Normandy, under the cover of darkness.

By maintaining pressure on the Germans, Montgomery kept them off balance thus preventing Rommel from extracting his panzer divisions from the line and forming an operational reserve. In addition, Hitler's insistence that there should be no withdrawal to more easily defensible lines and that 'positions were to be held at all costs', was a severe limitation to his field commanders.

12th (*Hitlerjugend*) SS Panzer Division

Amongst those panzer formations already facing the Allies in mid-June, was the *Hitlerjugend*. It had been in action since D+1 and was holding a ten-mile stretch of line west of Caen. The *Hitlerjugend*, or as Allied propaganda had portrayed it the 'Baby Division', was one of the newer German formations, raised in the aftermath of the disastrous capitulation of Sixth *Armee* at Stalingrad. In February 1943, Himmler wrote to the Reich

Plan No.1 from Army Group B (19 June 1944 for the planned counter-attack by Panzergruppe West.

A poster advertizing military training for the Hitler Youth movement

Teenage SS motor cycle reconnaissance troops belonging to the 12th (Hitlerjugend) SS Panzer Division.

Youth Leader:

> *'I have submitted to the Führer your offer, on behalf of the youths born in 1926, to form a division of volunteers for the Waffen SS to be of the same value as the* Leibstandarte. *I have also informed him of your desire and request that this division ... clearly emphasizes its origins and its simultaneous membership in the HJ.'*

The Führer duly approved a plan whereby 16,000 volunteer members of the *Hitlerjugend* youth movement (HJ) would report to pre-military training camps between May and July. Also released from service with the *Wehrmacht* were 2,000 HJ leaders who, with experienced SS veterans, mainly from the *Leibstandarte*, were to form the nucleus of the Division. SS-*Oberführer* Fritz Witt, was to command the 12th SS *Hitlerjugend* Division, which was officially formed on 1 June 1943. Almost exactly a year later the Division proved to be, arguably, the most effective German formation fighting in the west.

Forming an élite division from scratch was not easy, particularly as the *Hitlerjugend* had to train itself. To ease the situation, fifty *Wehrmacht* officers joined the division to fill certain key posts for which the *Waffen* SS were unable to provide suitable trained and experienced officers. Weapons, vehicles and all kinds of equipment were in short supply, even for the SS, who were increasingly taking the cream of the Reich's production. Many recruits reported for duty in their HJ uniforms and those who transferred from the *Wehrmacht* or the *Luftwaffe* continued to wear their old uniforms for some time. Training was entirely orientated towards battle, with little emphasis on foot drill and other traditional elements of military discipline. As *Divisionsadjutant* SS-*Sturmbannführer* Springer explained:

SS-Oberführer Fritz Witt. The first commander of the newly formed 12th (Hitlerjugend) SS Division.

'Priorities during training [were]: 1: Physical fitness. 2: Character development. 3: Weapon and combat training.'

Unit training took place in Belgium, but despite shortages of equipment, ammunition and fuel, the HJ volunteers, were developing into high quality eighteen year old soldiers.

In April 1944, the *Hitlerjugend*, now a fully fledged panzer division, moved to billets between the Orne and Seine, taking the place of 10th (*Frundsberg*) SS Panzer Division, which had been rushed east to face the

Soviet's spring offensive. Here it completed its training and provided 2,042 surplus soldiers to the *Leibstandarte*. This fostered even closer links with its sister formation, which it was now, in theory, grouped with as a part of I SS *Panzekorps*. Following an inspection of the *Hitlerjugend*, in a report dated 1 June 1944, SS-*Obergruppenführer* Sepp Dietrich declared:

'The Division with the exception of the Werfer Battalion and the Panzerjager Battalion, is fully ready for any action in the west.'

The words of eighteen-year old SS *Sturmmann* Leykauff reveal the state of the Division's morale on the eve of the invasion:

'Everyone was waiting for the attack across the Channel. We were fully aware that decisive battles were approaching. Our first action lay ahead. We were looking forward to it.

'The Allies planed to take apart the "Baby Milk Division", as they called us. But we were not afraid. Sometimes we even got carried away a bit, and big-headed. After the intensive training on our weapons, we felt sure we could take the heat. It had been said that the enemy would be physically superior to us. Well, we knew that we were quick, agile and confident. We trusted our officers and NCOs who had been hardened in battle. We had known them since the beginning of training. During combat exercises with live ammunition we had enjoyed seeing them in the mud together with us, with steel helmet and submachine gun.'

SS-Obergruppenführer Sepp Dietrich was able to report that the new division was ready for action.

Before dawn on D-Day, the *Hitlerjugend* stood-to but spent most of the day waiting. Despite repeated requests from *Armygruppe* B and Seventh *Armee*, OKW only released the division at 1430 hours. However, moving at 1740 hours, it was repeatedly attacked by fighter-bombers. The leading elements of the Division came into action west of Caen and quickly established a reputation amongst their British and Canadian opponents for having an uncompromising determination in battle that verged on fanaticism. Allegations of war crimes, such as the murder of sixteen Canadian POWs, in the days immediately after the invasion did much to shape the nature of future fighting with the *Hitlerjugend*.

Casualties suffered by the *Hitlerjugend* in the two weeks after D-Day

Motor cycle recce troops of the Hitlerjugend Division arriving near Caen, June 1944. These eighteen year olds head towards the coast and their first action watched by Wehrmacht infantry.

Below and opposite: Photographs taken during the Hitlerjugend's first battle against the Canadians.

were high but on a relatively static front, lightly wounded soldiers were evacuated and eventually returned to their units, while armoured vehicle casualties were recovered for repair or cannibalization. Thus, the number of soldiers and equipment available to face Operation EPSOM at the end of June was higher than the *Hitlerjugend's* raw casualty figures would indicate.

Lieutenant General Sir Richard O'Connor (left) commander of VIII Corps, consults with his superior, General Sir Miles Dempsey, commanding British Second Army.

The British

VIII Corps's arrival in Normandy had been badly delayed by the Channel storm that raged from 19 - 22 June and dangerously slowed the Allied build-up, while giving the Germans an opportunity to balance the forces in Normandy. Lieutenant General Sir Richard O'Connor had performed spectacularly in the early desert campaigns before being taken prisoner. He had escaped and was given command of VIII Corps by Montgomery. His command had very few Regular Army soldiers and few veterans of the desert or Mediterranean in its ranks. Most of VIII Corps's troops, the Infantry of 15th Scottish and 43rd Wessex, together with the tanks of 11th Armoured Divisions, were originally part-timers of the Territorial Army or were war raised units. However, after five years of war, there was little distinction between units manned by Regulars, Territorials or conscripts and in Operation EPSOM, they were to fight their first, long awaited, battle of the war.

15th Scottish Infantry Division had originally been raised as a New Army division in the Great War. Its divisional sign had been an 'O' – the fifteenth letter of the alphabet but following an inspection, King George VI suggested that the arms of Scotland be inserted into the badge.

'On 2nd September 1939 the 15th Scottish Division was reborn. It had been begotten by national necessity out of 52nd Lowland Division.

'The business had started that spring, when, with a wave of his magician's wand the Secretary of State for War, had duplicated the Territorial Army. Unfortunately, Mr Belisha had omitted to duplicate with the same gesture the Territorial Army's equipment, accommodation and training facilities.'

In the run-up to war, existing Territorial battalions provided cardres for new units, as volunteers flocked to the colours in a manner reminiscent of 1914. Many of the volunteers were old soldiers, whose military experience eased the problems of training. Initially the 15th was based in towns scattered across southern Scotland. However, by the

VIII CORPS

43rd Wessex   **15th Scottish**

11th Armoured

end of September the Division was concentrated in the Borders, living in mills in Galashiels and Hawick. In October, 'essential workers' taken back by the Ministry of Labour and men not meeting new medical standards, were replaced by English recruits from the Midlands 'who soon became Scottish as the Scots'.

As the Battle of France in 1940 reached its climax, 15th Scottish moved south to face Hitler's expected invasion of the Essex coast. As the invasion scare receded, the emphasis increasingly swung to training but by autumn 1941, the manpower demands of the fighting in the Middle East forced the Division to become a 'Lower Establishment' formation. Men, units and even 45 Brigade left the Division during 1941 and 1942. However, in December came the news that the Division was to be built back up to 'Higher Establishment', which was reached by April 1943 and shortly afterwards the Division joined VIII Corps. Men posted to the Division, which now included conscripts from across the UK, were soon taking part in increasingly complex exercises on the Yorkshire Moors.

Suspicions that the Division was to take part in the Second Front were confirmed when General Montgomery visited and addressed units from the bonnet of a jeep. In common with other invasion troops, the King and Mr Churchill also visited 15th Scottish Division. In April 1944, the 15th moved south to begin the process of waterproofing and final training. The Division started to arrive in Normandy on 13 June but the storm of 19 – 22 June badly disrupted the Division's arrival.

EPSOM's second major formation was 11th Armoured Division, commanded by the experienced and successful thirty-seven year old Major General 'Pip' Roberts. This division had been formed in March 1941, largely from Territorial units such as the 2nd Fife and Forfar Yeomanry (F & F Y) and newly raised units such as 23rd Hussars (23 H). The 11th Armoured went through many changes of ORBAT and was in both reality and rumour frequently 'just about to go overseas'. However, the Division was destined to train and retrain as tactical doctrine and equipment changed with regularity. Officers pawed over reports from the Mediterranean and exercise authors sought to reflect the latest tactics in exercises on the increasingly familiar training areas of Stanford in Norfolk and the bleak Yorkshire Moors.

With late arrivals such as the veteran 3rd Royal Tank Regiment (RTR) being incorporated into 29 Armoured Brigade, the Division moved to Aldershot for waterproofing. After a long wait, 11th Armoured Division landed in France on 13 and 14 June. However, it was another ten days before it tanks made their way forward to Operation EPSOM's assembly areas.

The only veteran formation to take part in the operation was 4 Armoured Brigade, whose black and

4 Armoured Brigade.

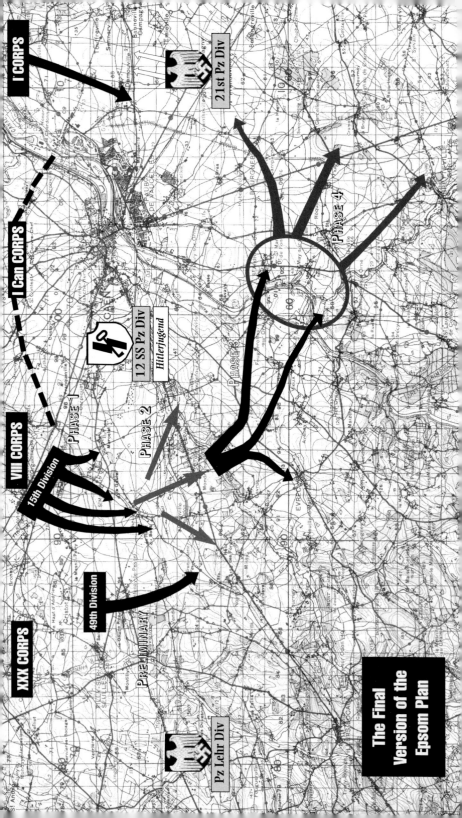

The Final Version of the Epsom Plan

white desert Jerboa flash was worn on the battle dress of its soldiers. Originally raised as the Heavy Armoured Group of the Mobile Division (later 7th Armoured Division) in Egypt, 4 Armoured Brigade had been an 'independent' formation since 1943 and had fought in the desert, Sicily and Italy. The Brigade was one of those favoured formations, selected by Montgomery, to return to the UK to spearhead the invasion. It consisted of old Regular Army units; the Scots Greys and 2nd Kings Royal Rifle Corps (2 KRRC), a Territorial unit 3rd County of London Yeomanry (3 CLY) and a war raised unit, 44 RTR. This mixed military heritage did not matter a great deal, after years of practical experience of war in the Mediterranean. Landing on D-Day, the Brigade had two weeks of fighting behind them, making them in all respects the most experienced formation fighting during EPSOM.

The EPSOM Plan

On 18 June, Montgomery issued Directive M502 to his army commanders, Generals Bradley and Dempsey, to whom he gave, respectively, the 'immediate task' of 'the capture of CHERBOURG' and 'the

Generals Montgomery and Bradley photographed during their planning meeting 22 June 1944.

capture of CAEN'. In his direction to Second British Army, he envisaged that: 'The operations against CAEN will be developed by means of a pincer movement from both flanks'. Initially Montgomery intended that VIII Corps would deliver the main attack, east of the River Orne, on 22 June, following four days of attack by I and XXX Corps to the west of the city. However, as detailed planing began, it became obvious that a corps could not assemble in the tight bridgehead east of the Orne without the British intentions being all too obvious. The following day an amendment, M 504, was issued:

'It has therefore been decided that the left wing of the of the pincer movement, from the bridgehead over the ORNE, shall be scaled down and be only of such a nature as can be done by the troops of I Corps already there.

'VIII Corps will be switched to form part of the right, or western wing of the pincer movement ... The final objective of VIII Corps will remain as given in para 12 of M 502 [Bretville-sur-Laize], but the Corps will advance to this objective on the general thrust line:

ST MANVIEU 9269 – ESQUAY 9460 – AMAYE SUR ODON 9757.

'... The above operations will begin at or about dawn on 22 June. VIII Corps will be launched on its task on the morning of 23 June.'

The storm that battered the Normandy coast seriously delayed the Allied build-up and gave the Germans some respite.

However, the storm that was already doing its best to destroy the Mulberry Harbours, seriously disrupted the landing programme and delayed the start of the preliminary operation east of the Orne until 23 June. The initial attack west of Caen began on 25 June and the main EPSOM attack, by VIII Corps, the following day.

The limited attack from the Orne Bridgehead, by 51st Highland Division, was designed to force the enemy to commit 21st Panzer Division and its reserves to this area. While the aim of the preliminary attack by 49th West Riding Division, on 25 June (Operation MARTLET), was to unbalance the enemy and to seize the Rauray Spur which dominated VIII Corps's area of operations. General O'Connor considered it vital, if EPSOM was to succeed that the Spur was cleared of enemy. Supported by 8 Armoured Brigade and advancing parallel to VIII Corps, 49th Division's subsequent objective was to secure the Noyers area. On VIII Corps's left, I Canadian Corps would mount operations to capture Carpiquet, once the breakthrough was well established.

In making his EPSOM plan, General O'Connor considered the difficult ground across which his troops were to attack. From their start line, the attackers would have to negotiate, what the official historian described as:

'... an area of wide hedgeless fields of standing corn [wheat], falling slowly to the Mue, an insignificant stream. From there southwards the landscape is more typical of the bocage, its small farms and orchards enclosed by thick and steeply banked hedges, its villages half hidden in hills and its outlines broken by woods and coppices. From the south west a ridge [the Rauray Spur] of higher ground extends across the battlefield with spurs running northwards towards Fontenay le Pesnel and Rauray on XXX Corps front and on VIII Corps towards le Haut du Bosq with a final hump [Ring Contour 100] south east of Cheux.'

Beyond Cheux was a belt of excellent defensive ground, which presented the enemy with cover and good fields of fire. Once through this area of bocage, a string of villages along the Caen to Villers-Bocage road offered the German more good positions from which it would be difficult to dislodge them. Beyond the road, the ground dropped sharply into the Odon Valley. This valley had precipitous wooded sides and the river itself had steep tree-lined banks together making it a serious obstacle to armour. To make matters worse, there was only one crossing on the main axis at Tourmauville. Therefore, engineers would be needed well up in the advance to improvise additional crossings for armoured vehicles.

Rising out of the close confines of the Odon Valley was the broad open plateaux of Hill 112. This feature is visable from much of the area west of Caen but it is not until standing on its upper slopes that its dominating position is fully appreciated. From Hill 112, a series of ridges sweep down

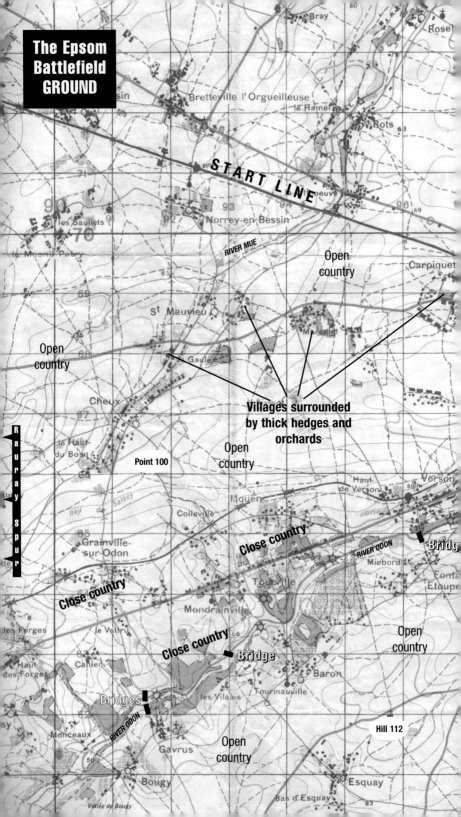

The Epsom Battlefield GROUND

Bray

Rosel

Bretteville l'Orgueilleuse

le Hamel

Rots

START LINE

les Saullets

Norrey-en Bessin

RIVER MUE

Open country

Carpiquet

St Mauvieu

Marcelet

Open country

Gaule

Cheux

Villages surrounded by thick hedges and orchards

le Haut du Bosq

Point 100

Open country

Rau de Salbey

Mouen

Haut de Verson

Verson

Rauray Spur

Colleville

Grainville-sur-Odon

Close country

RIVER ODON

Bridge

Mieberd

Tourville

Fonta Étoupe

Close country

Mondrainville

des Forges

le Valtru

Close country

Bridge

Open country

Cahier

Baron

Haut des Forges

les Vilains

Tourmauville

Bridges

RIVER ODON

Monceaux

Gavrus

Hill 112

Bougy

Esquay

Bas d'Esquay

Vallée de Bougy

to the valley of the River Orne. Beyond this valley lay the temptingly open country that offered good going towards VIII Corps's objective at Bretville-sur-Laize.

The second factor that General O'Connor considered was the enemy. SS *Standartenführer* Kurt Meyer's 12 *Hitlerjugend* SS Panzer Division held ten miles of the front, from Fontenay-le-Pesnel, east to Carpiquet, across the N13 and on to the north east of Caen. Consequently, the *Hitlerjugend* were deployed in positions that lacked depth. VIII Corp's intelligence sections believed that SS-*Obersturmbannführer* Mohnke's 26 Panzer Grenadier Regiment (26 Pz Gr) that held positions between Fontenay-le-Pesnel and east to the N13, 'amounted too little more than a well developed outpost line'. It was here that the British were to attack. So long was 26 Pz Gr's sector that all three battalions were in the line, along with 12 SS Pioneer Battalion (12 SS Pi) who were under command. Unlike the British, the Germans considered their assault/field engineers to be a fully-fledged combat arm and expected to perform in close combat alongside.

Behind the infantry was SS-*Obersturmbannführer* Max Wunsche's 12 SS Panzer Regiment (12 SS Pz Regt), with its two battalions dug-in in blocking positions, having also reconnoitred counter-attack options. A return dated 24 June 1944 reported the number of tanks operational: fifty-eight Panzer IVs and forty-four Panzer Vs (Panthers). This significant tank force was backed up by the guns of 12 SS Artillery Regiment and seventeen heavy anti-tank guns. The Division's Chief of Staff, SS-*Sturmbannführer* Hubert Meyer, in sumarizing the *Hitlerjugend's* design for battle, explained that the artillery:

> '... was in position behind Regiment 26 and depended on good co-operation with it, had also prepared for close defence and were well camouflaged. Because of the width of the sectors of the panzer grenadier companies, their positions did not have much depth. So the heavy infantry weapons, the panzers and the artillery were to form the strong points of the main battlefield.'

In the *Waffen* SS, no matter what the soldier's employment, he was expected to be above all an effective frontline soldier.

Deployed to the north of the Odon, were four companies of dual purpose 88mm guns belonging to 4 *FlakSturmregiment* and the *Hitlerjugend's* only uncommitted reserve: the half-tacks and armoured cars of the Divisional Reconnaissance Battalion. This battalion had a limited infantry capability and only a light armoured punch. However, in response to intercepts of VIII Corps radio traffic, I SS *Panzerkorps* moved two companies of 56-ton Tiger tanks belonging to 101 *Schwere* Panzer Battalion, into the area behind 26 Pz Gr as *Korps* reserve.

26 Pz Grs had held the front that the British were to attack since 15 June and, as SS-*Sturmbannführer* Hubert Meyer, recorded:

'In addition to the fox holes, positions for riflemen and machine guns had been set up in houses. The positions for the heavy infantry weapons had been carefully selected, camouflaged and prepared for close defence. Mine barriers and barbed wire obstacles had only been set up to a minor extent ...The *Pioneerbataillon* had reinforced its positions in a particularly expert manner. Despite the shortage of time, strong points for light and heavy infantry weapons had been established through extraordinary efforts.'

The British had, however, amassed a considerable force that was expected to sweep through what appeared to them to be a 'lightly held crust'. Nominally, VIII Corps had 60,000 men under command for Operation EPSOM but some, such as 43rd Wessex Division, were only just landing and assembling on 25 June. The Corps, including its own artillery, the guns of the flanking corps and the heavy, medium and field artillery regiments of the 8th Army Groups Royal Artillery (AGRA), had approximately 736 guns in support. This gave a concentration of a gun for every sixteen yards of attack frontage. Also included in the firepower equation were the ships of the Royal Navy. The monitor HMS *Roberts* and three cruisers were able to add their considerable weight of fire, as the battlefield, eighteen miles from the coast, was

The Epsom Battlefield ENEMY

Allied Front Line

German Front Line

44 Brigade

46 Brigade

la Villeneuve

Norrey-en-Bessin

25 SS Pz Gr

Carpiquet

I/26 SS Pz Gr

St Mauvieu

Marcelet

12 SS Pi

la Gaule

II/26 SS Pz Gr

Cheux

le Bijude

Haut du Bosq

Haut de Verson

Verson

Mouen

Colleville

uray

Grainville-sur-Odon

II/12 SS Pz (-)

88mm FLAK/ATk GUNS

12 SS Recce Bn

Miebor

well within range of naval guns. Finally, 250 heavy Royal Air Force bombers were planed to open the attack and 'cab ranks' of fighter-bombers would be on call above the battlefield.

VIII Corps's attack was to be delivered in four phases. Firstly, by two brigades of 15th Scottish Division advancing through positions held by 3rd Canadian Division, on a frontage of just 5,000 yards. The brigade groups consisted of their three normal infantry battalions and their artillery regiment, joined by the Churchills of 31 Tank Brigade and 79th Armoured Division's specialist assault armour. H-Hour for Phase One was to be 0730 hours, two hours after dawn, which would allow plenty of daylight for accurate bombing and observation of the artillery's 'fall of shot'.

See map page 22

15th Scottish

In Phase One, two battalions of 44 Lowland Infantry Brigade, supported by two Squadrons of 9 Royal Tank Regiment (9 RTR) were to advance on the Division's left flank, across the open fields of the Mue valley, and take St Mauvieu and le Gaule. On the right, two battalion of 46 Brigade, supported by two squadrons of 7 RTR, had further to advance on the right to take the straggling villages of Cheux and le Haut du Bosq. Waiting behind 15th Scottish Division was 11th Armoured Division, with 4 Armoured Brigade under command.

From this point, in Phase Two, depending on the tactical situation, a 'mobile column' of 11th Armoured Division, spearheaded by recce Cromwells of A Squadron 2nd Northamptonshire Yeomanry (2 N Yeo), was to make a dash forward. They were to seize the Tourmauville Bridge, five miles into enemy territory. At the same time, 15th Recce Regt would advance

11th Armoured

and cover the left flank in the area of Mouen. Meanwhile, in recognition of the difficulties that the Odon Valley presented to armour, 227 Highland Brigade was to advance with two battalions up, supported by two squadrons of Churchills, seize the line of the Caen to Villers-Bocage road. They were then to clear the Odon valley in detail. Subsequently, they were to take over defence of the bridges at Tourmauville and Gavrus,

In EPSOM's third phase, 29th Armoured Brigade was to press on across Hill 112 towards the Orne with, if necessary, the help of 227 Brigade. Meanwhile, 44 and 46 Brigades having been relieved by 43rd Wessex Division, would take over defence of the villages on the northern slope of the Odon Valley between Granville and Mouen. 15th Recce Regt was then to advance south west across Hill 113. In the fourth phase, 46 Brigade would cross the Odon and relieve elements of 11th Armoured Division in the Evrecy area. 4 Armoured Brigade had a number of options but its main objective was to cross the Orne and establish a bridgehead with 159 Infantry Brigade. If possible, it was to drive across the open 'tank country' to Bretville-sur-Laize, thus completing the envelopment of Caen from the west.

Fontenay

Caen-Fontenay Road

Rauray

The Germans' view from the edge of Rauray looking across the ground that 46 Brigade would advance on the first day of EPSOM.

Infantry of the York and Lancs Regiment moving through the northern part of Fontenay on 25 June.

le Mensil Patry

Cheux

le Haut du Bosq

46 HIGLAND BRIGADE

Following behind the Scots was the newly arrived 43rd Wessex Division. Its planned role, as explained by Brigadier Essame, was relatively simple:

The task of the Division was to follow the 15 (S) Division, taking over each objective as soon as possible after capture so as to enable the advance to be continued. The Commander emphasized the importance of St Manuvieu on the [open/unprotected left] *flank.'*

43rd Wessex

While VIII Corps was assembling for it's 'storm delayed attack', German armoured formations were approaching their own concentration areas for 'the drive to the sea'. However, as SS *Sturmbannführer* Hubert Meyer recounted:

'A meeting took place on 24 June at Panzergruppe *West. Taking part were ... XXXXVII Pz Korps and I and II SS* Panzerkorps. *They were briefed on the operations. No one knew that the preparatory attack for the British operation Epsom would start the next day and that the race to assemble had already been lost. The decisions taken too late from the very first day of the invasion onward had caused our reinforcement to lag behind by fourteen days. A German offensive on 20 or 21 June* [during the storm] *would have caught the enemy at a moment of extraordinary weakness.'*

In Operation EPSOM, the Allies struck first. It was a blow that the Germans were forced to react to and the opportunity for *Panzergruppe* West to seize the initiative was gone.

Operation MARTLET

Before considering Operation EPSOM, it is necessary to briefly examine the 'preparatory' attack mounted by 49th West Riding Division on the Rauray Spur, as this is essential to the understanding of battle as a whole.

31

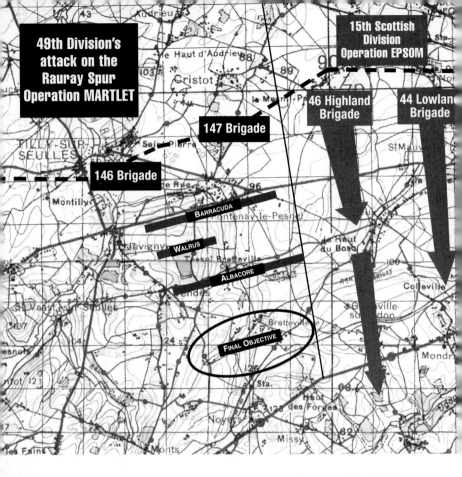

The Rauray Spur, over looking the ground across which VIII Corps was to attack, needed to be taken in order to deny the German the tactical advantage of dominating positions. However, at the operational level, MARTLET was also designed to 'unbalance' the enemy. This was to be achieved by forcing the Germans to commit their reserves, which would be 'fixed' in battle with the 49th Division when the main EPSOM blow fell.

Major General Barker had ample time to plan MARTLET in detail, as his Division was already holding the front from which he was to attack. His plan was to attack on a frontage of two brigades between Tilly-sur-Seulles and le Parc de Boislonde. In this stage, known as 'Phase A – Code word BARRACUDA', the 49th would take the village of Fontenay-le-Pesnel lying at the northern tip of the Rauray Spur. In 'Phase B – Code word WALRUS', 146 Brigade would advance across the Caen – Caumont Road. Its objectives, the northern edge of Tessel Wood, Point 111 and la Grande Farm, lay a mile to the south. The plan for 'Phase C – Code word ALBACORE', was for 147 Brigade to complete the immediate operation by seizing the Rauray Spur, while 146 Brigade would advance and protect the Division's exposed right flank.

49th West Riding Division

The 49th's attack was to fall on the junction between two German formations, the *Hitlerjugend* and the Panzer *Lehr* Divisions. Panzer *Lehr* had been formed by the *Wehrmacht* Panzer School from instructors and staff and was considered to rank amongst the premiere panzer divisions. One commentator said that 'When this division arrived in Normandy it was probably better equipped than any other German division during the war.' After a week in combat, on the eve of MARTLET, Panzer *Lehr* Regiment had a total of sixty-three Mark IVs and Panthers operational, with almost as many waiting in workshops to be returned to battle over the coming days.

Operation MARTLET was eventually set for 25 June, three days after the end of the storm. With settled weather, artillery gun positions received truck after truckload of ammunition, as supplies again flowed ashore. All two hundred and fifty guns within range were to fire in support of 49th Division.

Operation MARTLET – 25 June

The British artillery barrage began and, at 0415 hours, Phase A

Scottish infantry moving up at the start of Operation EPSOM.

(BARRACUDA) began with three infantry battalions, supported by Shermans of 24 Lancers, following a creeping barrage through the standing corn. Almost immediately the attackers were engulfed in a 'dense smoke laden mist. Visibility dropped down to five yards and unit commanders began to loose control.' Infantry platoons lost their way and crossed boundaries into other battalions' area, which added to the confusion.

Disorganized, the British ran into the SS and *Wehrmacht* panzer grenadiers, who had turned the thick, stone walled houses of Fontenay-le-Pesnel and surrounding farms into fortified strong points. Having lost the barrage, the advance was soon well behind schedule. Two battalions eventually reached their objective on the Caen – Tilly Road to the west of Fontenay. However, 11 Royal Scots Fusiliers (11 RSF), tasked to clear the village, encountered determined resistance from 3rd Battalion, 26 SS

A 25 pounder of the 49th Division dug in and camouflaged firing during the attack on Rauray.

Panzer Grenadier Regiment (III/26 SS Pz Gr). At 0815 hours, the reserve companies started fighting through the village but bitter hand to hand fighting in the buildings sapped the Fusilier's strength and they dug in around the Calvary in the northern part of Fontenay.

By late morning, the mist had burnt off and the Germans counter-attacked. 12th SS Panzer Regiment (12 SS Pz Regt), supported by SS-*Obersturmbannführer* Monke's panzer grenadiers, launched the most significant attack from the east. The SS advanced down hill towards the village. However, the 49th's anti-tank guns knocked-out the two leading Panthers as they advanced on Fontenay but a third panzer, remaining in cover destroyed one of the British anti-tank guns. A single Sherman was summoned and the remaining Panther was hit. Unsupported, the panzer grenadiers did not press home their counter-attack.

Phase B (WALRUS), had originally been scheduled to start at 0600 hours but the barrage that was to precede 1st/4th King's Own Yorkshire Light Infantry (KOYLI) eventually began at 1215 hours. Advancing up hill, through a checkerboard of banks, ditches and hedges towards their objective on the northern edge of Tessel Wood, the KOYLI suffered seventy-five casualties. The Yorkshiremen dug-in and managed to beat off a serious *Hitlerjugend* counter-attack from the direction of Rauray.

Back in Fontenay, 7 Duke of Wellingtons (7 DWR or the 'Dukes'), whose original mission was to take objectives south of the village, were instead tasked to clear the southern portion of Fontenay. H-hour was to be 2100 hours and the village was to be cleared by nightfall. This was largely achieved but the Germans were left holding some houses and woods to the east of the village.

Operation MARTLET had not succeeded in taking Rauray and the spur that still lay a mile to the south. However, the aim of sucking German reserves to face the West Riding Division's attack was succeeding. Overnight SS *Standartenführer* Kurt Meyer was ordered to concentrate 12 SS Pz Regt against the threat posed by the West Riding Division, despite his claim of severe misgivings.

MARTLET – Dawn 26 June

Operation EPSOM was not to start until 0730 hours, which gave 49th Division two hours of daylight to complete Operation MARTLET by seizing the Rauray Spur. Major General Barker's plan was for 8 Armoured Brigade, along with the Tyneside Scots, to attack south west from the gap between Tessel Wood and Fontenay, across the River Bordel towards Rauray. Meanwhile, 7 DWR was to resume its advance south from Fontenay and take St Nicholas Farm.

The *Hitlerjugend's* overnight regrouping had produced a coherent front and the 'Polar Bears' (49th Div.) were denied the generous artillery support of the previous day during the attack on Objective ALBACORE. However, 24 Lancers and the infantry of 12 Kings Royal Rifle Corps reached the outskirts of Tessel Bretteville but another armour/infantry battlegroup failed to take the bridge near la Grande Farm and the Dukes failed to take St Nicholas Farm. This left the Lancers and KRRC dangerously exposed to the fire of the Panthers of 1st Battalion 12th SS Pz Regt and they were withdrawn. Maj Stirling of the 4th/7th Dragoon Guards wrote:

> *'... this was a wretched day. The scene at the start-line was described as "a badly organized partridge shoot" because the infantry and tanks did not get lined up properly and our tanks were fired at by the infantry. C Squadron was overlooked from two sides. Two to six Tigers and Panthers were operating on the dominating high ground. On the left flank was a small wood in which four Tigers were sitting – cleverly placed so that it was impossible to get at them.'*

By midmorning, the 49th Division had made very little ground. The failure to clear the Rauray Spur meant that, from the north east edge of the broad spur, panzers and artillery observers were able to enjoy views across Cheux to the EPSOM start line. The 60,000 men of VIII Corps were to advance into the guns of the *Hitlerjugend*.

CHAPTER TWO

The First Day – St Manvieux and Cheux

It began to rain on 25 June, as the Scottish infantrymen, along with their supporting tanks, started to move forward from their concentration areas. Some troops arrived in Normandy and went straight into Orders Groups (O Gp) for their first operation, as a result of the delay the storm imposed on the landing programme. In the worst case, some of the Divisional Troops were landing as the battle started.

Trooper Les Arnold, a gunner in one of 9 RTR's two artillery observation post (OP) tanks, recalls the move to the Forward Assembly Area.

> *'Infantrymen from 15th Scottish Division were moving up accompanied by their pipers; they could be heard for miles and cheered us up considerably. During the evening we moved down towards the start line nose to tail with very little light; I remember we passed close to a railway line and just missed driving into an anti-tank ditch.'*

A Piper of 7 Seaforth Highlanders leads his company forward through the mist behind the leading Brigades.

Lieutenant John Stone commanded one of the significant number of armoured vehicles that broke down *en route* to the Forming up Point (FUP). Having been repaired:

'We clanked along slowly and lonely, following the "route up" signs.
... Suddenly from a ditch on the side of the road a Canadian voice
"Pick". Obviously a challenging password; what to answer? "Shovel"
I said. "Axe, you stupid bastard", was the tender reply. We clanked on
and eventually reached the Squadron two hours before stand-to.'

Lieutenant Robert Woollcombe of 6th (Border) Battalion The King's Own Scottish Border Regiment (KOSB) described the lot of the infantry on the night of 25 / 26 June.

'Arriving from Secqueville into the forward assembly area at 3 a.m.
in the drizzling rain. Pitch dark with the minute hand slipping leadenly
to dawn. Dug shallow pits as a precaution against enemy counter
shelling, and huddled with my batman, head to toe, with our anti-gas
capes spread over us for some warmth. Then more fitful sleep, until at
5.30 the sentries stole around the silent positions with muttered words,
shaking inert figures on the ground back into consciousness.

'We woke dully, shivering. Still dark, and the drizzle still falling,
with two hours to the barrage. ...Then a subdued jangle of mess tins, the
occasional glow of a cigarette end, and a straggling queue of men with
slung rifles: shadowy blurs forming for porridge, compo [tinned
composite rations] *sausages, biscuits and tinned margarine, and a*
mug of steaming tea, in the first glimmer of dawn.'

With the arrival of dawn, the rain stopped for a time but was replaced with a mist that rose from the low ground and enveloped the battlefield. Conditions for fighter-bombers were marginal over Normandy. According to the official history:

'On June the 26th flying weather was so bad in England that the
large programme of air support for the opening of EPSOM had to be
cancelled [at 0645 hours] *and, for the first time since D-Day,*
practically no aircraft based in England left the ground. Only 83
Group, stationed in Normandy, would be able to help VIII Corps, and
though they flew over five hundred sorties their support was
handicapped by low cloud and mist.'

Unaware that the bombing was cancelled, platoon commander Lieutenant Woollcombe wrote about the final stages of battle preparation:

'Green camouflage cream was shared out in grubby palms and
smeared over our faces. Weapons were carefully cleaned and oiled.
Magazines loaded bayonets fixed. Midday rations – slabs of bully beef
and cheese with more biscuits – packed into haversacks. The boiled

Morning of 26 June 1944, soldiers of 10 HLI moving up with their capes ready in case of further rain.

sweets and chocolate stowed into a handy pocket. Cigarette tins into another. ... the men quietly chatting and smoking in little groups. Everyone was admirably controlled, but an air of tension about them. None quite knew what battle would be like, as we waited for H-Hour.'

The Opening Barrage

It will be recalled that Montgomery had assembled 736 field, medium and heavy guns for EPSOM or sixty-four guns per kilometre, including the Rauray area, of attack frontage. The historian of 15th Scottish Division recalled the opening of the battle:

'As H-Hour approached the suspense was extreme. At 7.29 A.M. the orders came over the Tanoy speakers to the waiting guns: "Stand by to fire Serial 1 [of the fire plan] – one minute to go – 30 seconds – 20 seconds – 10 seconds – 5, 4, 3, 2, 1, FIRE." With an ear splitting crack hundreds of guns hurled their shells overhead, the infantry and tanks advanced to close up to the opening barrage line, where our shells were bursting 500 to 1000 yards ahead. It was the moment for which the 15th Scottish Division had been preparing for five years.'

Nowhere was the wait for H-Hour more tense than amongst the infantry

Tanks of A Sqn, 9 RTR, advancing from the battered church of Norrey-en-Bessin.

Norrey-en-Bessin and its rebuilt church today.

lying in the open in the wet corn. Lieutenant Woollcombe recalled:

'The minute hand touched 7.30 ... On the second, nine hundred guns of all calibres, topped by the fifteen inch broadsides from the distant battleships lying off the beaches, vomited their inferno. Concealed guns opened fire from fields, hedges and farms in every direction. During short pauses between salvos, more guns could be heard further away. ... It was like rolls of thunder, only it never slackened. ... Hurling itself

Gunners of 15th Scottish Division prepare to fire a barrage of 25 pounder shells.

A 4.5" gun belonging to 48 Field Regiment RA, in action at dawn.

The railway line south of Bretteville used as the Operation EPSOM start line.

onto strongpoints, enemy gun areas, forming up places, tank laagers, and above all concentrated into the creeping mass of shells that raked ahead of our own infantrymen, as thousands of gunners bent to their task.'

On the receiving end of the barrage was the *Hitlerjugend*. Its Commander SS-*Standartenführer* Kurt Meyer described what it was like:

'The earth seemed to open and gobble us all up. All hell had been let loose. I lay in a roadside ditch listening to the noise of battle. There was no let up to the artillery barrage. All telephone lines had been destroyed and communications with Divisional Headquarters and units at the front no longer existed... My ears tried unsuccessfully to analyze the

View from the railway bridge towards Marcelet and St Manvieu. 6 Royal Scots Fusiliers supported by 9 RTR advanced across these fields.

A troop of Churchills moving across the open ground in support of 15th Scottish Division.

One of a series of photos taken by Sergeant Laing of 15th Scottish Division's infantry moving forward through the corn and mist.

sounds of battle and all I heard was the permanent spitting, cracking and booming of the bursting shells, mixed with the noise of tank tracks.'

The barrage 'stood for ten minutes on the opening line', which coincided with the outpost line of the *Hitlerjugend's* defensive position, while the British infantry and tanks moved forward from their FUP and crossed the start line into battle.

St Mauvieu and le Gaule

44 Lowland Brigade was to attack on EPSOM's left flank. 6 Royal Scots Fusiliers (6 RSF), the same battalion that Winston Churchill commanded during the First World War, accompanied by the tanks of B Squadron 9 RTR, was to attack St Manvieu. Meanwhile 8th Royal Scots (8 RS or '8 Royals'), with A Squadron 9 RTR, had objectives astride the Caen-Fontenay Road and around the hamlet of le Gaule.

The attack did not start well for 6 RSF, as the only start line they could find was in a sunken road 125 yards from the opening barrage. This close to their own artillery fire, inevitably some rounds dropped short and, even with the cover of a sunken road, they suffered casualties from their own fire. In addition, two of the accompanying tanks from B Squadron were immobilized, having lost tracks on anti-tank mines near the start line, which had probably been laid by the Canadians. Such 'friendly fire' incidents are all too common during battle.

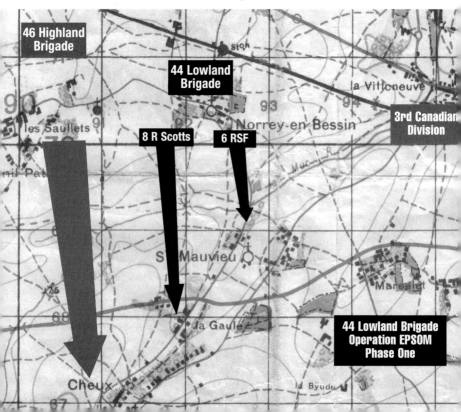

Another unexpected factor was that the dawn mist was replaced by the smoke of the barrage, which produced 'conditions almost of a fog-bank'. So thick and unexpected was the 'fog' that keeping direction across the open fields of corn clothing the slopes of the shallow Mue Valley was a problem. However, a problem of far greater significance for the Fusiliers was enemy mortar and artillery fire. 12 SS Artillery Regiment's observers, overlooking the area of the attack from Carpiquet, directed their own guns to fire at unseen targets just behind the British barrage. 9 RTR Trooper Reg Terrington, 8 Troop commander's radio operator, recalled:

'We crossed the start line and after a short while we were in the middle of a substantial barrage of shells. We couldn't tell whether they were ours or theirs but either way it was most unpleasant. My Troop Commander, Peter Beal, told me afterwards that I looked a bit green but I was still smiling. He looked the same.'

Unprotected by armour, to add to their earlier woes, 6 RSF continued to suffer heavy casualties from the bursting shells. Crossing the Mue, they continued to advance, closely following the barrage through the *Hitlerjugend's* outpost line towards St Mauvieu, which they reached at 0830 hours. At 1030 hours, the infantry eventually broke into positions held by I/26 Pz Grs around the straggling village and orchards of St Mauvieu. However, this was only achieved with the support of the demolition guns mounted on the AVREs of 81 Squadron, 6 Assault Regiment RE. The Fusiliers had suffered such heavy losses from artillery fire that their capacity for fighting through and mopping-up was greatly diminished. Meanwhile, the Churchills of B Squadron 9 RTR enveloped the village and engaged targets for the infantry. Even though they did not enter the village, three Churchills were recorded, in the war diary, as being knocked out at St Manvieu.

Lying just behind I/26 Pz Gr Regt's main line of resistance, SS *Sturmbannführer* Krause had established a strong point of mutually supporting positions in St Manvieu. Sheltering in the strongly built cellars, they quickly recovered from the powerful British bombardment, occupied battle positions, and continued to resist all day.

The *Hitlerjugend* had not only prepared the stone houses for shelter and defence but had also dug alternative positions in the surrounding orchards, hedgerows and farm buildings. In the words of the Scot's divisional historian: 'Very confused fighting in the village went on throughout the day'.

SS-*Sturmmann* Aribert Kalke recorded the defender's experience:

'The artillery fire was constantly increasing, finally concentrating on the centre of the village. Explosions hit the front yard, directly ahead of the entrance to the command post. The house was shaken by hits.

The bridge over the River Mue on the outskirts of St Manvieu. The Mue just about becomes a stream in the winter.

Between the explosions, we could hear the short, harsh barking of tank guns. The Battalion staff had sought cover in the cellar. Only a few men had remained in the upper levels. Radio contact with the companies had been lost... a messenger from 2 Kompanie *dropped into the command post through the smoke and fumes. He was wounded... and reported [that] the* Kompanie, *engaged in bitter hand-to-hand fighting, had*

Infantrymen of 6 RSF photographed on the morning of 26 June 1944 in St Manvieu.

been overrun. The enemy had broken through... and the enemy were concentrating strong tank and infantry forces against 1 Kompanie. Enemy tanks were immediately outside the command post.

'*SS-Sturmbannführer Krause ordered his adjutant to establish contact with a panzer Kompanie located in the la Byude area [a mile south] and request a counter-attack immediately. When the artillery fire slackened a little, three of us left the command post by a rear exit at short intervals. A small dense wood offered us cover... We found ourselves in a grain field, which also gave us cover from being spotted ... and we reached 9 Panzer Kompanie. The Kompanie commander categorically declined a counter-attack, as without accompanying infantry, panzers were not suited to fight in streets. Untersturmführer Holzel set up a new strong point with a few stragglers.*'

Meanwhile, back in Battalion Headquarters at St Manvieu, a German war corespondent reported the battle and an act of heroism:

'*Heavier and heavier, the shells from the tanks hammered the Chateau's park. The beams of the houses were splitting, bricks were flying from the walls. The earth was trembling. ... For almost three hours, they lay salvo after salvo on the line of main defence outside St Manvieu and the village itself. Foxholes were filled in, machine guns smashed and men were mercilessly ripped apart.*

'*The enemy broke through the positions and overran St Manvieu. Like a pack of hungry wolves they surrounded the village. The handful of men in the battalion command post could count fifteen Shermans [sic]. ... Whoever had weapons left to fight with was sent into action in the village, messengers, clerks and orderlies.*

'*... The Battalion command post had suddenly become an important bastion – and it had no heavy weapons, only sub-machine guns and rifles, with Panzerfausts and magnetic mines. But there were two mortars still sitting in the village and their crews had twenty-five bombs left. These they fired amongst the oncoming infantry and tanks, causing confusion. SS snipers crept to the hedges and walls and fired at the [British tank] commanders who came out of their hatches too soon.*

'*Some of the tanks turned away. They assumed the strongpoint to be much stronger and did not dare break in. But the calm did not last long, as the tanks returned and fired from all barrels. They picked the house as their target and damaged it so badly that the wounded had to be carried out.*

'*Then there was a shout of alarm within the doggedly defending platoon. A flame thrower tank was dominating the path to the command post. "That tank has to go" ordered the commander.*

Buildings used as a strong point in the centre of St Manvieu and as HQ of 1 26 Pz Grs.

'Unterscharführer *Durr had heard the order. He did not hesitate. "I'll go" he said. He took a* Panzerfaust *and went to scout the situation. It was difficult to get close to the tank, as it was dominating the terrain on three sides. '*Unterscharführer *Durr jumped across the inner wall of the yard and ran straight at the tank and fired. But the* Panzerfaust *did not pierce the tank. Maybe he had not aimed accurately enough in his excitement.*

'*He was hit! Shot in the chest. Angry, Durr pulled himself up, ran back and picked up another* Panzerfaust *and ran up to the tank again. This time he aimed at the tracks, which ripped. Again, Durr was the*

A section commander and two riflemen belonging to 6 RSF in St Manvieu.

target off violent machine gun fire. Crawling, he worked his way back. He spotted a magnetic mine and quickly grabbed it. A comrade wanted to hold him back.

'For a third time he set out. He ran, stumbling, towards the tank, paying no attention to the bullets. He attached the charge and was about to get away when the charge dropped to the ground. He grabbed the mine, pressed it against the tank as it exploded.'

SS-*Unterscharführer* Emil Durr was recovered from beside the knocked-out Crocodile, while the British had temporarily withdrawn. However, he died of his wounds four hours later. Durr was the first *Hitlerjügend* NCO to be awarded the Knight's Cross.

Not all of the *Hitlerjugend* fought so tenaciously. Trooper Les Arnold recalled how:

'The infantry captured some Hitler Youth soldiers who came swaggering into our lines; this attitude annoyed us particularly because

Britain's answer to Germany's finest, escorts these two members of the Hitlerjugend to the rear and interogation by a VIII Corps intelligence officer.

Officer of the Hitlerjugend being interogation by a VIII Corps intelligence officer.

we had heard that some of their units had shot Canadian prisoners'.
Despite the loss of several Crocodiles, the strongpoint based on Battalion HQ I/26 Pz Gr was eventually flamed by 141 (The Buffs) Regiment Royal Armoured Corps. However, small groups and even individual *Hitlerjugend* continued to fight on all day and into the evening.

To the west of the Fusiliers, 8 Royal Scots formed up with A Squadron 9 RTR and crossing their start line, closed up behind the artillery barrage and followed it towards the Caen-Fontenay Road and the hamlet of le Gaule. Initially the Royals were able to keep up with the barrage, which advanced at the rate of a hundred yards every three minutes. However, the survival of enemy riflemen and *Spandau* teams, along with the fire of the *Hitlerjugend's* artillery and mortars slowed them considerably.

Consequently, the British artillery barrage moved on ahead, allowing time for the young SS soldiers to recover from the numbing effect of exploding shells and engage the advancing Scotsmen in the standing corn. The troop of Crocodiles was of considerable help in subduing determined resistance.

8 RS eventually reached the Caen-Fontenay road, two thousand yards from their start line, at 0930 hours, two hours after H-Hour. However, within an hour they had reached their objective and cleared le Gaule, and were digging in as fast as they could. The Royal Scot's thrust had benefited from inadvertently striking the boundary between I/26 SS Pz Gr and 12 SS Pioneer Battalion to the west, which is traditionally a weak point in defensive positions. VIII Corps war diary recorded that:

'It appeared that the village [le Gaule] *was firmly in their hands, but numerous points of resistance were still being doggedly defended and had to be fought. This fact and a number of counter-attacks made the situation less favourable than initial reports indicated.'*

Lieutenant Woollcombe was waiting with 6 KOSB, as 44 Brigade's reserve, south of Norrey:

'Crump!... Crump!... Crump!... Crump!... German shrapnel airburst. "Get down – stop walking about!" We lay for about ten minutes, watching the airbursts over some tall trees in the orchard. More appeared over Norrey. Then stray figures in battle-dress materialized out of the mist, coming back from the battle. Each with levelled bayonet prodding two or three helmetless and sullen bewildered youths in grimy camouflage smocks and trousers. They held their hands in a resigned and tired way, above their blond heads.

'A miracle anything could have lived through the stunning

Heavy laden infantry advancing through the mist. Note how pouches are stuffed full, carrying extra bandoliers of ammunition and their jacket fronts contain extras.

bombardment they had taken, and a testimony to the efficiency of the slit trench.'

One company of 6 KOSB was sent to help the Royals, while three companies were to be dispatched to St Manvieu. 'Then Colonel Ben's word came over the wireless. Gavin relayed us the signal.... "The Battalion will advance". We arose and moved up the field in extended line of sections.' During their advance, 6 KOSB came across small groups of panzer grenadiers in the corn or hedgerows who had been missed by the Fusiliers. Most surrendered promptly and were taken to the rear. Lieutenant Woollcombe recorded one surprise meeting:

'Suddenly we froze at a burst of fire from Black's Bren gun, firing from his hip, and instantly an apparition rose screaming from the corn and rushed towards us, throwing itself at my feet. It was an SS soldier.

'... But he was in no state for offensive action, by a neat bit of shooting by Black, who had hit him in the shoulder. He knelt at my feet clutching my knees, frantic with pain and terror.

'"Don't shoot – don't shoot – have pity" He knew that much English. We understood. To key up their resistance they had been told the British shoot all prisoners. He now expected death in cold blood. ... We carried him into the Company position.'

Most of the Borderers now saw their first dead bodies; 'khaki clad Fusiliers and camouflaged Hitler Youth, whose tender age was a surprise to many'.

6 KOSB arrived in St Manvieu, where the process of clearing the village, its trench systems, dug-outs and rubble was slow. Lieutenant Woollcombe recalled entering the village:

'A number of dulled men in steel helmets, wearing anti-gas capes against the rain were discovered in a captured German position: Scots Fusiliers, twenty eight of them, all that was left of a company that had crossed the start-line that morning. The company commander was dead and a tired captain with handle bar moustaches was in command. ... He had been reduced to a state of fatalism and recited to me their losses in a strain of mournful satisfaction.'

For the Scottish infantry it was a long day's fighting in St Manvieu before they would finally crush the *Hitlerjugend* and be relieved.

Cheux and le Haut du Bosq

Having seen that his front south of Fontenay was holding against 49th Division's assault, 'PanzerMeyer' raced back to his Headquarters in Verson where he received two messages. The first was from I/26 SS Pz Gr Regt. 'The battalion was being attacked by strong forces. All attacks on St Manvieu had been repulsed up to that point.' However, the second message was more disturbing.

Sappers making their way forward through the mist, having been summoned to breach the Hitlerjugend, minefields.

'The chief of staff [SS-Sturmbannführer Hubert Meyer] was still holding the telephone handset in his hand and reported: "That was our last conversation with the Pioneer Battalion commander". He had reported: "Enemy artillery have destroyed my anti-tank defences. The battalion is being overrun by British tanks. Individual positions are still holding out around Cheux. Enemy tanks are trying to crush my dugout. Where are our tanks? I need a counter-attack from the direction of the Rau..." at that point, the line was cut. Radio communications had also been destroyed.'

12 SS Pioneer Battalion's (12 SS Pi) HQ was positioned on 'a small hill immediately south of the road Caen – Fontenay, half a mile west of le Gaule', in the centre of 26 Pz Gr Regt's sector. It was were being attacked by 46 Highland Brigade's left assault battalion, 2 Glasgow Highlanders (2 Glas H), supported by fifteen Churchills from A Squadron 7 RTR. The Brigade's right assault battalion, 9 Cameronian was attacking II/26 SS Pz Gr along with the tanks of B Squadron. The 'Funnies' of 79th Armoured Brigade supported both battalions.

46 Brigade had advanced only to find that, 'Within a quarter of a mile of the start line, the forward battalions ran into a minefield. Despite casualties from anti-personnel mines, the rifle companies went on through, but the advance of the supporting Churchills and AVREs was held up'. The

A Churchill of 7 RTR moving through a marked minefield gap on the morning of 26 June. Note the marker post to the left.

flails of B Squadron 22 Dragoons came forward and beat a path forward at one and a half MPH. The belt of minefields laid by 12 SS Pi had achieved its tactical aims extremely well. Not only did patches of mines and anti-tank fire covering the obstacle belt cause nine armoured vehicle casualties, it also slowed the tempo and cohesion of 46 Brigade's attack from the outset. Exacerbating the resulting confusion was a failure of the No.38 sets to communicate effectively between tanks and infantry, which led to further separation of the two arms. In addition, the creeping barrage moved on and even a fifteen-minute dwell on the Caen-Fontenay Road was not enough for the Brigade to catch up. Consequently, until a route through or round the minefields could be found, the infantry of 46 Brigade were without tank or artillery support.

Even with the delay caused by the minefields, VIII Corps's Intelligence summary records that a *Hitlerjugend* prisoner taken in the outpost line, said when the barrage started: 'We had gone to ground and had emerged only to find ourselves surrounded by tanks or furious Scotsmen throwing grenades'. However, factors other than enemy defences were at work reducing the 15th Division's military efficiency. Chief amongst these was the mist and with a greater distance to their objectives, navigation was more important for 46 Brigade. Private Hamish McDougal of 7 Seaforth, following behind the leading battalions explained:

'All I could see was two or three mates each side of me as we walked

into that cornfield and heard our tanks moving. Before long we heard small arms fire, but with the fog we had no idea where it was coming from, or in fact if we were still going in the right direction. I heard the Lieutenant blow his whistle a few times to give us a clue where he was, but that stopped and we heard bangs as the tanks ran onto mines. Next we heard shouts and hadn't a clue what was going on, but then suddenly, shells were landing amongst us.'

On 46 Brigade's left was 2nd Glasgow Highlanders (2 Glas H), whose objective was Cheux but to reach it, they would have to fight through 12 SS Pi's well-prepared defensive positions. The pioneers had used all their field-engineering skills to prepare deep shelters that were both well camouflaged and effectively sited. Consequently, many of the SS soldiers survived the barrage and were missed by the first wave of attacking infantry and armour. Appearing from their bunkers, they either shot into the rear of the leading wave of Scots infantry or engaged subsequent waves with rifle, *Spandau* or *Panzerfaust* fire. VIII Corps' war diary described the German reaction in the centre of the attack:

'The enemy was holding his positions and let us pass when he was not directly attacked, overwhelmed or overrun. He only revealed himself when presented promising targets or had himself been spotted. There were numerous points of resistance, which had to be cleared long after objectives had been reached, in the forward as well as the rear areas ... It was remarkable that in all cases, that the enemy in these positions fought until the defenders had been killed or the positions captured.'

In many cases, the battle

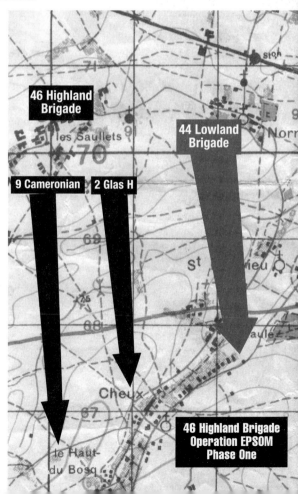

Kurt 'Panzer' Meyer

Hurbert Meyer

had totally bypassed isolated individuals or groups and, in several instances the *Hitlerjugend's* signal log recorded radio contacts with groups that had been overrun three days earlier. Others managed to infiltrate back to their own lines under cover of darkness. One of these was the commanding officer and HQ staff of 12 SS Pi, who had last been heard of, with a tank attempting to crush his HQ dugout, at around 0900 hours. SS-*Standartenführer* Kurt Meyer recalled that:

'*SS-Sturmbannfuhrer Muller himself defended his command post against all the enemy attacks. A captured pioneer was finally sent into the bunker to ask his comrades to surrender. He preferred to stay there and share his comrades' fate. The attack continued past the command post after demolition attempts had badly shaken the bunker and it looked like a mass grave. The survivors finally fought their way to our lines at about midnight. They were found completely exhausted at le Haut du Bosq, after having decided to take a short break.'*

Behind the SS Pioneers' main line of resistance, Cheux had been developed as a strongpoint. Defences were based on a battery of II/12 SS Panzer Artillery Regiment's towed 105mm guns and 12 SS Pi's supply platoons acting as infantry. 2 Glas H had a difficult advance, with elements of the battalion becoming lost in the fog, while others fought their own private battle with small groups of *Hitlerjugend*.

Private Angus Jones was amongst the Glaswegians lost in the fog:

'*... and it rained like hell and we all got fed up – it was all very different to what we had expected. As soon as we reached some ruins at the edge of Cheux, we set up for defence and waited for orders, but none came until a Sergeant Major we didn't know ran up and said, "Don't hang around lads – get on!" So we did, moving from house to house, under fire from Jerries we couldn't see. There were shells and mortars and small arms fire zipping and banging around us and a lot of blokes never made it.'*

A number of SS pioneers, who had escaped the battle on the main line of resistance, joined the SS gunners

Floods and battle damage in Cheux 27 June 1944.

Rebuilt Cheux.

and supply troops led by two staff officers, SS-*Untersturmführer* Asmus – a technical engineer officer, and SS-*Untersturmführer* Lorenz – a supply officer. They fought from hedgerow, to house, to pile of rubble, as 2 Glasgow Highlanders fought through the ruins of Cheux. It was a protracted and bloody business, with mounting casualties on both sides. The fighting on the first day of EPSOM, which was also their first day in action, cost the Glasgow Highlanders twelve officers and nearly two hundred men.

With furthest to advance, 9 Cameronian had objectives in le Haut du Bosq but first they had to breakthrough II/26 Pz Gr's main line of resistance. They were hardly across their start line before they came under artillery fire. SS-*Oberscharführer* Hans Hartmann of 5 *Batterie* II/12 SS Pz Arty Regt, positioned between le Haut du Bosq and Cheux, recalled how he engaged the Cameronians and the tanks of 7 RTR with his 105mm field guns:

The Mark VII Churchill of the type used by 7 and 9 RTR of 31 Tank Brigade. This example can be seen on Hill 112.

'*In the morning, our commander advised us that the Batterie OP was being abandoned. Thus, we were on our own. I went to the football field in front of us and climbed onto a goal. Approximately 4 Km away, south of le Mensil, I spotted an assembly of some twenty enemy armoured vehicles. We started an engagement with all four guns. It was so well aimed that the tanks dispersed in no time. Judging by the explosions, one tank must have taken a direct hit. As the vehicles pulled away, they stirred up so much dust that we could no longer observe anything.*'

Resuming their advance, the Cameronians had expected that 49th Division would be protecting the right flank, having taken the Raury Spur.

However, the West Riding Division's attack had failed and the Cameronians were exposed to flanking fire during the final stage of their advance to le Haut du Bosq.

Despite artillery fire, minefields and continued 'sniping', the Cameronians continued to advance and were nearing le Haut du Bosq at 1100 hours. However, the hamlet had also been developed into a strongpoint based on two batteries of guns of I/12 SS Pz Arty Regt and Regimental HQ of 26 SS Pz Gr Regt along with its specialist platoons. Led by SS veterans, the *Hitlerjugend* were in well prepared positions that they were not going to give up without a fight. Under fire from *Spandaus* and anti-tank guns, the Cameronians were checked on the open slope up to le Haut du Bosq. They went to ground, while the Churchills of 7 RTR duelled with the anti-tank guns. However, help was at hand in the form of the Crocodiles of 141 Regt RAC. Lieutenant Andrew Wilson described a typical Crocodile flame mission:

> 'Suddenly the hum of the headphones cut out. It was the Squadron Commander calling us forward. We were going in to flame.
>
> 'At the start of the first rise Barber was waiting with the infantry CO. He made an up and down movement with his clenched fist, which was the sign for opening the nitrogen bottles on the trailers.
>
> '"Got where we are?" said Barber, pointing to the place on his map. His finger moved to an orchard four hundred yards away stayed there a moment, then moved to a field beyond it. "There are some Spandaus there. Flame them out. The infantry will follow you. A troop [of tanks] is waiting to cut off the enemy at the back" I wanted to ask: "How do you spot Spandaus?" But it sounded too silly. With the other troop leaders, I ran back to the tanks. The crew were closing the trailer doors. "Mount I shouted. They climbed in and slammed down the hatches.
>
> '"Driver advance. Gunner, load HE." The troops moved forward in line abreast, mine was on the left. As we came through a hedge, mortaring started. Everywhere infantry were crouching in half dug foxholes, trying to protect their bodies from the bursts of the bombs.
>
> 'We went through a couple of fields. Any moment now we should see the orchard. I reached down and put on the switch, which let up the fuel into the flame gun. Suddenly it came into view: a bank of earth, another hedge, and beyond it the orchard. "There you are. Dead ahead driver." The driver slammed into second gear. The tank reared up for a moment, so you couldn't see anything but the sky; then it nosed over the bank,

and through the periscope I was looking down a long empty avenue of trees. Somewhere in this avenue, someone was waiting to kill me. "If only I knew what to look for?"

'My sergeant and corporal moved their tanks alongside mine. I ordered, "Co-ax [coaxial machine gun], *fire" but there was no target to indicate. The gun roared filling the turret with bitter fumes which made my eyes smart. Through the periscope, I saw the other troops start to flame, the yellow fire sweeping through the trees. "Better get my own flame going. Flame gun, FIRE".*

'I heard the hiss, the slapping like leather of the fuel striking the target. The fuel shot out, spraying the trees, paving the ground with a burning carpet. The tank ran on through it. "Slap it on, flame-gunner, all you've got!" The flame leapt out with an almost unbroken roar. The driver was slowing up, uncertain where to go.

'Suddenly the leader of the other troop called across the wireless: "Hello Item Two. Don't go into this lot. Let them have it from where you are." I saw nothing but blazing undergrowth. Surely, no one would have dared to stay there. But I kept the troop at the edge of the field, pouring in the flame, till the fire rose in one fierce, red wall.

'Then the gun gave a splutter like an empty soda-water siphon. The other troop had finished, so I turned my tanks and followed. Beneath the trees with smouldering leaves, the British infantry were coming in with fixed bayonets. I never saw the enemy!'

The Cameronians burst through the burning hedgerows of le Haut du Bosq and at 1130 hours, they reported that they were mopping-up their objective. None the less, the Cameronians suffered casualties (dead, wounded and missing) totalling six officers and one hundred and twenty men, or the equivalent of an entire rifle company.

To complete EPSOM's first phase, 7 Seaforth, hitherto 46 Highland Brigade's reserve, was to advance from Cheux and occupy the exposed Ring Contour 100, some 1,500 yards to the south east. The feature, a broad 'rounded hump' was held by a mixed bag of SS panzer grenadiers and other arms who had been pushed out of their positions during the morning. In addition, the first German reinforcement to the EPSOM sector, 15 Recce *Kompanie*, 25 Pz Gr Regt was just beginning to arrive. However, the Seaforth had been badly delayed in its advance by artillery fire, bypassed enemy riflemen and by the chaos in Cheux, Lieutenant James Hayter explained:

'When we finally reached Cheux we were few and minus our tanks. There was nothing to see but mud, water, ruins, smoke and mist, and the air was alive with missiles. I tried to see how many chaps had made

A close up of the Churchills armourments. In the turret a 75mm gun and a coaxially mounted 7.92mm BESA machine-gun. A second BESA was fired from the tanks hull.

79th Armd Div

Infantry supported by a Churchill of 31 Tank Brigade advance through the mist and standing corn.

it, but this was difficult because of the conditions, but I knew that some were under cover. I lay amongst some redbrick ruins that were still quite hot to the touch. I carried a Sten gun and grenades; I had a Corporal close by and not far away two men with a Bren. All the rest were dead wounded or out of sight. Then we heard tanks but had no idea if they were theirs or ours. The noise was fantastic and I couldn't understand how a battle could be fought in such a condition of mist.

'But then the mist began to clear and I saw Jerries not far off. They wore brown jackets and were, I thought, trying to collect some of their wounded, so we didn't fire. Then some of our tanks [7 RTR] appeared and as they went by we gave them a wave. Two of these Churchills were brewed up, so we were again unsupported. Then the rain came down in torrents so we tried to hide under our capes, but had to stay vigilant.'

At 1400 hours, 7 Seaforth was ordered forward to take Ring Contour 100. Lieutenant Hayter continued his account:

'... I'd lost my little compass and sense of direction. Then a Captain appeared in a scout car and told us the way before going off. But as soon as we started to move the Jerries let us have it with multiple mortars and all hell let loose. We were forced to get down in the rubble again and took a beating. Then came a pause in the enemy barrage and we were able to rush off out of Cheux in the direction

Young soldiers of the Hitlerjugend taking on the Allied tanks.

Unterscharführer Willy Kretzschman with his crew from 5 Kompanie II/12 SS Pz Regt. Note the fifteen kill rings on the barrel of their tank.

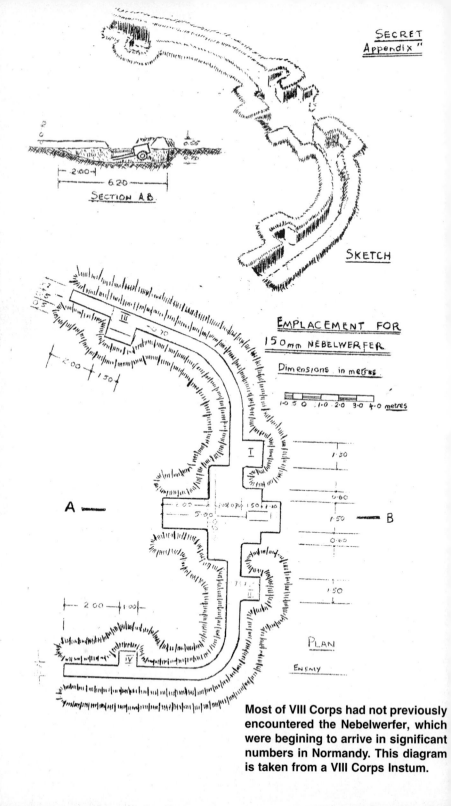

SECTION A.B.

SKETCH

EMPLACEMENT FOR
150mm NEBELWERFER

Dimensions in metres

PLAN

ENEMY

A

B

Most of VIII Corps had not previously
encountered the Nebelwerfer, which
were begining to arrive in significant
numbers in Normandy. This diagram
is taken from a VIII Corps Instum.

The Nebelwerfer's six barrels enabled the Germans to hit targets hard. Even if not hit, the scream of the bomb as it descended, did much to undermine the morale of men in the target area.

indicated and joined up with others of a different unit. The mist had thinned and we were getting fire from all directions, including mortars. I felt something nick my right leg, but I kept going. We reached the railway line, I believe, at Colleville, but didn't get any further that day, which had been a bad one.'

According to the divisional historian, advancing across the top of Ring Contour 100 or the Hump:

'The Seaforth found the reverse [southern] slope of the hump strongly held and failed to take it. After suffering fifty casualties,

including four officers, and losing several tanks, the Seaforth dug in north of the hump, leaving the crest as a no-man's-land between themselves and the Germans.'

With the capture of the villages of St Manvieu and Cheux and the northern slope of Ring Contour 100, 15th Division's Phase One objectives had been reached but villages and orchards were in the grip of 'sniper scares'. The Scots were already over three hours behind the schedule given in their operation order.

In summary, the skilful camouflage and thorough defensive preparations that the SS officers and senior NCOs had insisted on had paid off. The barrage had driven the SS to ground, only to appear as the leading Scots passed over them and unexpectedly engage the following companies. The cancelled heavy and medium bomber sorties would have collapsed bunkers and speeded the advance. However, bunker-busting delay fuses would also have cratered the ground, impeding armour/infantry co-operation. The delay in breaking through the *Hitlerjugend's* outpost and main resistance line bought 'Panzermeyer' valuable time to react, as will be seen in the next chapter.

A Tiger belonging to 101 Schwere Panzer Battalion moving to the front. Note the SS Panzerkorps emblem on the tank's hull.

CHAPTER THREE

The Armoured Battle and Infantry Stalemate

Before examining Operation EPSOM's second phase, it is necessary to briefly examine 49th Division's progress on the Raury Spur during the afternoon of 26 September. The battle on the spur was to have an important impact on 11th Armoured Division, which was about to advance on the main axis.

During the morning, lacking sufficient artillery support, 49th Division's renewed attack mounted by 8th Armoured Brigade and 7 DWR, had failed to dislodge the *Hitlerjugend's* armour. Having returned to the area of their start line, 7 DWR supported by the Shermans of the Sherwood Rangers Yeomanry (SRY) were to attack St Nicholas Farm at 1500 hours for a second time. This time the Dukes were successful: benefiting from both artillery support and the redeployment of a high proportion of *Hitlerjugend's*

A Company headquarters awaiting orders to advance on the afternoon of 26 June.

Regimental Headquarters of 44 RTR moving up during the afternoon of 26 June.

panzers to face the main EPSOM attack. Sensing a vacuum ahead of them, the SRY pressed on alone, up the ridge for a further mile to the Cheux – Tessel Road, halting five hundred yards short of Rauray. Unsupported they called for the infantry. Eventually, 11 DLI reached the SRY at 2100 hours and secured what was now a toehold on Spur's northern end

Phase Two – The Advance of 11th Armoured Division and 227 Highland Brigade

227 Highland Brigade and A Squadron of 11th Armoured Division's recce regiment, 2nd Northamptonshire Yeomanry (2 N Yeo), had been following up behind 46 Brigade ready to take over the lead as quickly and seamlessly as possible. The divisional plan was that the Cromwells of A Squadron would dash from the Cheux area to the Odon bridges and, following them, 227 Brigade would advance with two battalions and clear the Odon Valley. Meanwhile, 29 Armoured Brigade was to be ready to advance to the Odon and then across Hill 112 to the Orne.

On the left flank, 2 Gordons, (227 Brigade) supported by C Squadron 9 RTR, were to take Tourville and 10 Highland Light Infantry (10 HLI), with C Squadron 7 RTR, had Granville as their objective. Subsequently, 2 Argyle and Sutherland Highlanders (2 A&SH) would seize or take over the defence of the Odon bridges, while 11th Armoured Division continued the

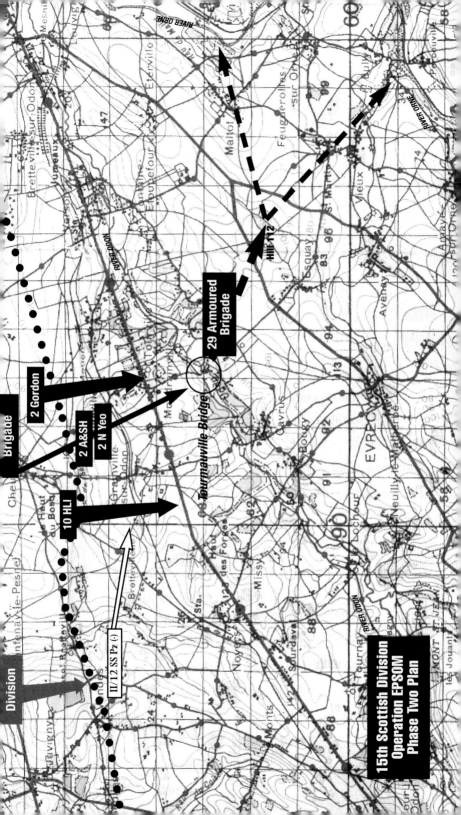

Brigade

2 Gordon

2 A&SH
2 N Yeo

10 HLI

Division

II/12 SS Pz (-)

Tournauville Bridge

29 Armoured Brigade

Hill 112

15th Scottish Division
Operation EPSOM
Phase Two Plan

advance into the depths of the enemy rear. 'It all sounded elegantly simple', commented an officer of one armoured regiment. However, 26 Pz Gr's determined defence north of the Caen – Fontenay Road had slowed 15th Scottish Division's tempo and enabled the *Hitlerjugend* to redeploy and prevent a dangerous gap being ripped in their lines.

SS-*Hauptsturmführer* Siegel's 8 *Kompanie* had been preparing to go back into action against 49th Division to the north of Rauray at midday on 26 June:

'Four panzer IVs, the only battle ready ones of the Kompanie, *were refuelling and being hastily filled to the brim with ammunition. Since early morning, the enemy had been pushing with more and more force against our lines, and the men hardly took time even for a swig from their water bottles. We had been in action for twenty-four hours already and the soldiers' faces showed the strain. Then* SS-Obersturmbannführer *Max Wünche arrives. He orders me to clear up a very recent enemy breakthrough south east of Cheux by a counter-attack, with these four panzers. "Situation is confused – there is no time to be wasted – no infantry available to cover you" – that was the gist of what he said.*

'A quick briefing of the crews, my panzer will lead. Then they mount. The engines howl, the hatches are pulled shut, barrels and turrets are swung into combat position. The last shouted good wishes from the Regimental commander are swallowed up by the clanking of panzer tracks.'

SS-Obersturmbannführer Max Wünche.

5 and 7 *Kompanies* of II 12 SS Pz Regt were also to deploy to face the new threat. They took up positions on the ridge to the south west of Cheux. Thus a potent force of over twenty-five Mark IVs was moving into place, just in time to face the armour of 29 Armoured Brigade and 31 Tank Brigade.

At the first sight of the British armour, to the west of Cheux and le Haut du Bosq, SS-*Hauptsturmführer* Siegel ordered his tanks to halt:

'We engaged these visible targets, and the enemy armour began to give off the well-known clouds of dark black smoke. Then, at top speed, taking advantage of the confusion our surprise intervention had caused, we raced across an open plain to the cover of a stand of trees at the bottom of a valley, and pushed on from there, firing all the time. Our

A Churchill and a section of anti-tank guns waiting to advance south on the afternoon of 26 June 1944.

A Section of Bren gun carriers belonging to 2 Glasgow Highlanders. Photographed near Cheux.

SS-Unterscharführer Otto Knot a tank commander in 5th Kompanie Hitlerjugend.

own artillery began to bring down defensive fire to help us, we contacted our troops on the left flank who cheered our arrival, and spread out to the right, eastward to close the gap broken in our line. Finally, we were in position on the eastward, or enemy side, of le Haut du Bosq, facing towards Cheux. Ahead of us, a wide and slowly rising meadow lies wide open, leading to the enemy. Behind it – distance approximately 1,200 to 1,500 metres – the gabled roofs of Cheux. We stop here, the panzers ready to fire.'

Siegler had re-occupied positions that he had been moved from to face Operation MARTLET. VIII Corps's war diary described that:

'There were many examples of enemy panzers being dug-in, and for each of these positions, there was an alternative position. These positions had been carefully chosen and prevent any close approach.'

As early as 1150 hours, VIII Corps approved orders for 2 N Yeo to dispatch A Squadron's Cromwell tanks to seize the Toumauville Bridge. Moving along the boundary between 44 and 46 Brigades towards the northern end of Cheux, the Squadron encountered a minefield that prevented them approaching the village from the north. Eventually entering the village, which was still being cleared by 2 Glas H, they came under fire from small arms, grenades and *panzerfausts*. 2 N Yeo's history describes the scene in Cheux:

'... it took A Squadron a considerable time to find a way through or over the heaps of rubble, shell holes, and burning buildings. They were met by many determined snipers and "Bazooka-men" in the orchards and demolished buildings, behind chicken-houses, high banks and hedges. Several Germans were shot while trying to climb on to tanks with grenades and magnetic mines.'

Infantryman Roland Jefferson of 8 Rifle Brigade (8 RB), 11th Armoured's Motor Battalion, accompanied the tanks into village: '

'We moved through the blasted ruins of Cheux and for the first time encountered being shelled ourselves. There was German sniper action and we had to seek them out and eliminate them. Perhaps for the first time, I realized that there was a vast difference between the text book soldiering when we were winning the battles on the Yorkshire Moors and the real thing we were now experiencing.'

Belatedly leaving the southern end of Cheux, shortly after 1300 hours, A

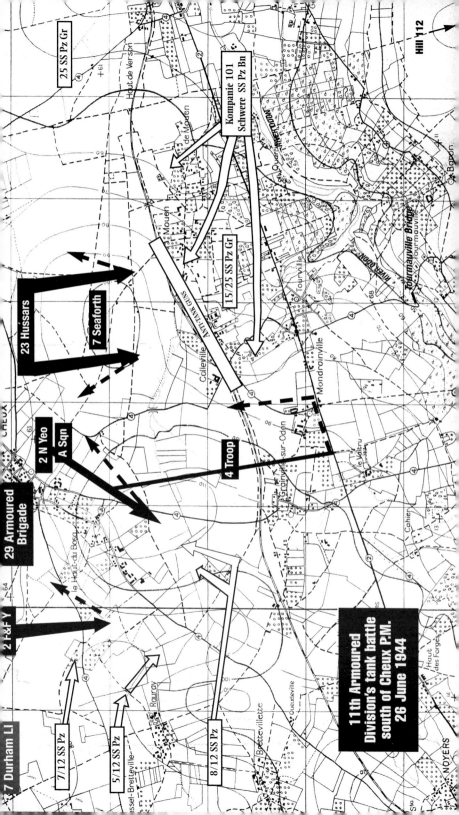

11th Armoured Division's tank battle south of Cheux P.M. 26 June 1944

A British Cromwell tank of the type used 2 N Yeo in the recce role.

Squadron 2 N Yeo had missed the supporting barrage, which was repeated at 1330 hours. Under cover of this fire, the four troops of Cromwells deployed astride the road *'but soon came against anti-tank opposition, suffered casualties, and reported that they were unable to go on'*. Reg Spittles was an A Squadron troop corporal:

> *'My troop [2 Troop] was sitting back in reserve. 4 Troop had gone on over the ridge to the left. 1 Troop and Squadron HQ's advance was halted by a deep ditch, so the only tanks I could see moving were 3 Troop on the right. I was idly watching them motoring up the hill just as if they were on exercise. I wouldn't have driven up so fast. Anyway, they went steaming up this slope. I suddenly looked back and two of the Cromwells were burning; knocked out. Major Peel came up on the radio and said you can see what has happened, get up there!*
>
> *As troop corporal, I led the way in arrowhead formation. Going steadily, I went up between the two burning Cromwells, hoping that the smoke would cover me. I stood up in the turret to see, over the crest with my binos. I couldn't see anything, so we trundled forward and I could then see these Mk IVs [Seigler's Company mentioned above], with a few Panthers amongst them moving in the valley across my front. These were what had hit 3 Troop's tanks. We sat up there firing and knocked out several Mk IVs. They fired back at us but as they were moving, they missed and they didn't seem to want to seriously engage us, just get across our front.'*

Supporting 2 N Yeo were the M 10 self propelled guns of 75 Anti-Tank Regiment RA. Sergeant Brettle recalled that he:

> *'... spotted a Mk IV brewing up the Yeomanry's Cromwells. It was*

lurking behind a house and I ordered the driver to start up and be ready to move. We fired but the muzzle smoke was a dead give-away. I saw a return AP cutting a path through the top of the corn crop and reversed smartly. My wireless operator could see through his periscope as the enemy AP sizzled past: "Curly – that was bloody close!" he calmly said.'

A Squadron, 2 N Yeo, Number 3 Troop was completely knocked out, as it attempted to cross the open ground and Reg Spittle's troop, along with 1 Troop, was pinned down and unable to make any progress. However, 4 Troop, under command of Lieutenant Stock, benefited from a more covered axis of advance and reached the railway line at Grainville at 1500 hours and advanced far enough to radio back a report on the state of the Odon valley and crossings. Having done that 'they spent a happy ten minutes shooting up a group of 20mm flak guns and their crews'. Despite this limited success, it was apparent that there was not going to be 'an elegant armoured drive' for the tanks to the Odon and beyond. According to the divisional war diary, 'A Squadron 2 N Yeo were ordered to pull out', as the *Hitlerjugend's* panzers had established blocking positions.

Tanks and soft skin vehicles of 23 Hussars are camouflaged in the hedgerow while the infantry flush out Hitlerjugend riflemen.

By mid afternoon, *Hauptsturmführer* Siegel's panzers were not only facing 7 and 9 RTR's Churchills, but also the Shermans of 29 Armoured Brigade. Major General 'Pip' Roberts, commanding 11th Armoured Division, who earlier had lost his own tank, at a crucial moment on a Canadian anti-tank mine, recalled:

'About 1230 hours I got orders to send 2nd Northants Yeomanry on their dash for the Odon Bridges, to be followed by 23rd Hussars, 2nd Fife and Forfar Yeomanry and supported by 3 RTR. But unfortunately no close infantry/tank mutual support for which the Division had trained for many years was possible.'

Hauptsturmführer Hans Siegel.

On the right, to the west of Cheux, were 2 F&F Y and in the open country to the east of the village were 23 Hussars (23 H). Neither Regiment had been in action before and 'The bocage country came as a great shock, it was all very different from the open country of our training areas in East Anglia'. Not least, because the Germans were making effective use of the cover afforded by hedges and sunken lanes.

Lieutenant Steel Brownlie of 2 Fife and Forfar Yeomanry (2 F&F Y) was to the west of Cheux and recalls his first advance:

'The regiment formed up 1,000 yards short of Cheux alongside a

Waiting Infantry men look on as a Churchill tank moves forward.

*regiment of Churchills of 31 Tank Brigade and an assault was made on
the village. C Squadron went straight in. We went left but were stopped
by tank ditches and sunken lanes, so were switched to the right. Don
Hall took his troop round the edge of a wood, myself following. Two of
his tanks went up in flames and he came roaring back, laying smoke
from the burning tanks. Two APs* [armour piercing shot] *came just
over my head so I too laid smoke and got out.'*

Lieutenant Robson of A Squadron 23 H was not so lucky. Leading his troop
forward onto a ridge south of Cheux, his Sherman was hit. The regimental
historian recorded that:

*'Those who witnessed it will always remember the shock of seeing for
the first time one of the Regiment's tanks go up in flames. One moment
an impregnable monster, ... forging irresistibly towards the enemy; the
next, a crack of a terrific impact, a sheet of flame – and then, where there
had been a tank nothing but a helpless, roaring inferno.'*

Deployed in good positions on the ridge between Rauray, Grainville and
Colleville, the SS panzers had halted the British advance but the pressure
exerted by three armoured regiments was telling on the Germans. SS-
Untersturmführer Willi Kandler a platoon commander of 5 *Kompanie*
recalled:

'Even as we approached, numerous enemy tanks of various sizes
[2F&F Y] *could be seen on the hill to our left. They had come from le
Mensil, in the direction of Cheux. Before we could turn into our old
position by the hedge, we became involved in a violent duel of the tank
guns, with successes and losses. Driving a few metres ahead of my
Panzer,* Untersturmführer *Buchholz was standing in his turret. His
panzer took a direct hit and Buchholz's head was ripped off. Since a
column of English tanks had already broken through, the* Kompanie
*withdrew, fighting, for two or three hedge-bordered pasture squares to
the south. We took up new positions on the route Cheux-Noyers. As I
recall,* Oberscharführer *Junge encountered, on the way to the new
positions, Sherman tanks that were advancing in a parallel direction. At
very close range he knocked out five of them.'*

The panzers were not the only *Hitlerjugend* troops moving back. SS
Sturmbannführer Muller's 12 SS Pz Arty Regt's positions in Cheux and le
Haut du Bosq had been overrun and as SS-*Standartenführer* Kurt Meyer
recorded that: 'The battalion was pulled back through the [centre] Sabley
sector'. However, the *Hitlerjugend* still held positions dominating the
routes south from Cheux.

To the east, beyond the blocking positions was the *Hitlerjugend's* HQ
Defence *Kompanie*. The divisional commander, SS-*Standartenführer* Kurt
Meyer, wrote a colourful account of 23 H's attack:

The crossroads north west of Cheux.

'*All command and control had become impossible. At that point, I could only be a soldier amongst soldiers. The eyes of the grenadiers lit up when they noticed me moving from section to section. These soldiers were unshakeable. They would not waiver or give way.*

'*Soon there was no piece of ground where a round had not exploded. Enemy tank rounds exploded in our lines. Our defensive area was reinforced by two tanks and an anti-tank gun. We clasped the few remaining* Panzerfausts *tightly to our bodies.*

'*A Panzer IV exploded and two Shermans were burning in front of us. The mass of enemy armour gave me the willies. Didn't it border on madness to try to stop this army of steel with a handful of soldiers and a few rifles? It was too late to speculate; there was only one thing left to do – fight!*

'*Two Shermans pushed closer down a defile. Some grenadiers lay in wait with their* Panzerfausts *behind blackberry bushes. I held my breath, and the exploding rounds had suddenly lost their terror. Spellbound we watched the soldiers as they got ready. The lead tank advanced further and further down the sunken road with covering tank rolling slowly behind him. It rolled past at that point; the second tank was as far as our soldiers .The barrels were pointed at Verson, but they would never fire again. A soldier rushed at the second tank. His* Panzerfaust *smashed into the Sherman's side. The tank rolled on a few meters then stopped, smoking. The lead tank had also been halted; it lost its tracks on mines. Two survivors surrendered.*

'*The Recce Company* [15/25 Pz Gr Regt] *fought for its life to my right. Wild artillery fire flung muddy earth high into the air. An anti-tank gun was still in position; it fired round after round into the British 11th Armoured Division's column of tanks. A British artillery barrage reduced the gun into a heap of scrap metal. There were no more serviceable anti-tank weapons and tank rounds shredded the company.*

'*I tried vainly to obtain artillery support. The spectre of "lack of ammunition" had been plaguing us for a long time. A couple of German artillery rounds were not enough to check the onslaught. The British tank attack continued. I knew every single one of these young soldiers, the oldest barely eighteen but they knew how to die!*

'*A new sound suddenly mixed into a hellish concert. A lone Tiger was giving us support. Its 88mm rounds gave the Shermans an unmistakable command to halt. The British tanks turned away; they called off their attack.*'

A handful of the powerful Tigers had arrived just in time to prevent a final breakthrough of the *Hitlerjugend's* position. Just how close VIII Corps was to success on the afternoon of EPSOM's first day is indicated by this paragraph written by Kurt Meyer:

'*We found two knocked-out British tanks on our return to the Divisional Headquarters; clerks had destroyed them with*

A Tiger of 101 Schwere SS Panzer Battalion.

Mid-day north west of Cheux. A Sherman belonging to the Fife and Forfar Yeomanry (29 Armoured Brigade), explodes dramatically. The flail belongs to B Squadron 22 Dragoons.

Panzerfausts. *The wrecks were less than 200 meters from the Headquarters. The HQ staff had dug in for all round defence.'*

Under pressure from the attack, 'Panzermeyer' recorded his feelings during the late afternoon of 26 June:

> *'The danger of a breakthrough by enemy tanks existed mainly south east of Cheux in the direction of the Odon crossing near Verson, or south of Tourville... The general command was constantly informed of the situation and was requested to send reinforcements. Initially, one company of the Korps Tiger Battalion was promised and moved to the area south of Cheux. Later SS-*Brigadeführer *Kraemer, chief of staff of I SS* Panzerkorps *advised that one company each of panzers and assault guns from 21st Panzer Division would be attached to the "HJ".'*

In addition, two battalions of 1st *Leibstandarte* SS Panzer Division's infantry had been tasked to join the *Hitlerjugend* but they were still a long way from the battlefield. However, placing of six of the eighteen operational Tigers under the *Hitlerjugend's* command had produced immediate results. The 56-ton monsters, positioned on the ridge around Grainville and Mondrainville, using their 88mm guns' 2,000 yard range, were able to cover routes south from Cheux and sweep Ring Contour 100, with both main armament and machine gun fire.

The Advance of 227 Highland Brigade

The armour having failed in the face of superior German firepower, it was the infantry who again were sent forward by Major General Macmillan. This time it was the Highlanders of 227 Brigade. The divisional historian recorded the Brigade's first move forward, at 1800 hours:

> 'From the forming up place, they set out southward through Cheux by two roads that lead to the Odon.

> 'Cheux they found a heap of ruins – its streets flooded and cumbered with fallen masonry. In it was the most appalling traffic jam. Vehicles were trying vainly to go in every direction at once, and no one seemed to be in charge. Moreover, the place was in the grip of an intense sniper scare, and indiscriminate firing was going on up and down the streets.'

With tanks closed down because of friendly and enemy fire, according to 15th Scottish Division's Military Police, 'they were deaf to the entreaties of infantry transport trying to move through Cheux'. This is a classic example of the results of two formations attempting to operate on a single axis on a narrow front.

Having shaken free of the traffic chaos, shelling and snipping, 227 Brigade's leading battalion, 10 Highland Light Infantry attempted to moved to its planned FUP south of le Haut du Bosq. However, they found it occupied by Siegle's panzers. In addition, they had parted company with their transport, including their mortars and machine guns, as well as 7 RTR's supporting Churchills. Sergeant Green describes 10 HLI's move up and the attack from the infantryman's point of view:

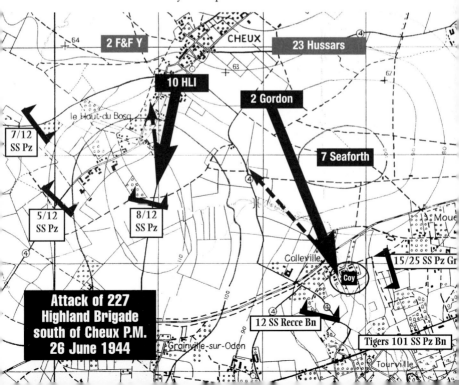

'It was late afternoon when we were ordered forward in extended order across the Caen road towards Cheux, every man keyed up and searching each fold in the ground for snipers, though as yet not a shot had been fired at our leading troops. When within fifty yards of the road, a young German in a camouflaged uniform rose up from the long grass almost under the muzzle of a Sten gun which killed him instantly. This was purely a nervous reaction on the part of the owner, and the only case I was to see of a German being killed for no reason. But it started a sniper scare and a lot of indiscriminate firing took place in all directions. The rain now came down with teeming ferocity... The orchard area of le Haut du Bosq was reached and we passed through the

forward troops of 46 Brigade, control was difficult, direction was lost in the orchards, and then we struck trouble. Machine guns opened up at the leading companies which, shocked by the suddenness of it, went to ground. Our supporting tanks replied, the tracer ricocheting in all directions, a source of fear to all and sundry, Scottish and German. Each time the leading companies tried to advance, they were met by heavy fire, and the advance petered out.'

The divisional historian wrote: 'Finding that a further advance was impossible in such conditions, Lieutenant Colonel Young concentrated the HLI in the southern outskirts of Cheux preparatory to a renewed advance at daylight.'

Meanwhile, on 227 Brigade's left, 2 Gordons, supported by C Squadron 9 RTR, formed up in the open to the east of Cheux, below the slopes of Ring Contour 100, held by 7 Seaforth. Although the Gordons had an easier time forming up than the HLI, they still suffered casualties from *Nebelwerfers*. Despite enemy fire, they advanced across the Sabley and up the ridge towards Colleville, with two companies forward covered by a creeping barrage. Sergeant Trevor Greenwood of C Squadron wrote in his diary:

Sergeant Trevor Greenwood, 9 Royal Tank Regiment.

'We took up our start position in a large field below the crest of a hill: 5.00 p.m. Our infantry were in position too, all smiling and cheerful. I think they were really glad to have our support. They asked us to swipe hell out of Jerry!

'Close to zero-hour, word came that sixty Panthers were on the move [rumour! There were no more than twenty-five Mk IV from II/12

SS Pz Regt on the ridge, supported by six Tigers]. ... *After about an hour, we commenced our delayed start at 6.15 p.m. Infantry ahead and rifles at the ready over the crest ... towards the woods where we knew there would be trouble. By 7.00 p .m. the battle was on.'*

Infantryman Private Jim Fisk was advancing on the Gordons's left flank:

'We were in amongst some trees, or what was left of them, and suddenly there was fire coming at us from all directions, including our rear. There were yells and curses and we all dropped to the dirt and mud and started shooting, though we couldn't see a thing, partly because of the mist, but also because the Jerries were so well hidden.'

Sergeant Hall, troop sergeant of 15 troop, came under fire at the same time in his Churchill called Ilkley.

'It started to rain and as we were approaching the ridge. On the right flank [10 HLI and 7 RTR] we saw some tanks had been hit and set on fire. I saw green tracer coming towards us, one passed to the left and one to the right. The third was a direct hit on the turret. We fired back along the ridge at what was either a Tiger or a Panther [Tiger or Mk IV: probably the latter] and reversed to be able to come up in a different position. This we did and ended up three-quarters on to him. We came under fire straight away and received several more hits, mostly on the hull. Because we were at

A commander's Panther moves up during Operation EPSOM.

NW

N

RAURAY

LE HAUT DU BOSQ

CHE

10 HLI

D170

GRANVILL

Panaroma showing the German view across the Ruisseau de Sabley from the ridge north of Granville.

an angle none of the shots penetrated the armour but when we tried to reverse before coming up onto the ridge in another position, we had lost hydraulics. As we were still under fire, it was only a matter of time before Ilkley was knocked-out.

'I gave the order to get out and we all met up in a nearby shell hole. We came under mortar and sniper fire, but due to the wet ground no one was hit although mortars landed very close. We walked back through Cheux and reported to the B Echelon vehicles.'

Despite casualties amongst infantry and tanks, the Gordon's battlegroup determinedly pressed on towards the railway line, which was held by the recently arrived troopers from Recce *Kompanie* 25 SS Pz Gr. The war diary of 9 RTR war recorded that:

'Continuous rain made it difficult to locate targets and gradually one tank after another became a casualty. C Squadron deployed so that half engaged the enemy tanks, while the remainder pushed on to help the Gordons.'

11th Armoured Division's war diary also recorded that,

'29 Brigade report they are helping to shoot attack into Colleville, but enemy tanks and guns prevent 31 Tank Brigade getting up to their infantry.'

Meanwhile, the Gordons were having trouble with mortars and snipers as they approached Colleville. However, eventually they reached the village. Private Jim Fisk describes the fighting:

'Then our Lieutenant got hit not far from us; he shouted at us to keep moving. So we did ... Then we saw some ruined houses – it must have been almost an hour later. I know I looked at my mate's watch and was surprised so much time had passed. We reached those houses with fire

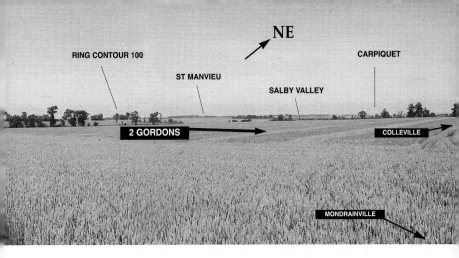

NE

RING CONTOUR 100   CARPIQUET

ST MANVIEU

SALBY VALLEY

2 GORDONS   COLLEVILLE

MONDRAINVILLE

coming at us from all directions and blokes falling down and calling for medics. There was a high grey wall and I huddled up against it with my mate and waited. We had no orders and didn't know which way to move. The battle got worse and we heard tanks and saw a Churchill moving along the street but it was hit and caught fire.'

Having broken into Colleville, the Gordons lacked the strength to hold the village and were eventually forced to withdraw under persistent mortar fire.

During the fighting in Colleville, the left assault company had become separated from the remainder of the battalion and was surrounded. It was assumed to have been wiped-out. According to RTR Sergeant Greenwood 'We were in action until it was too dark to see ... must have been 10.30 p.m'.

Trooper Jack Woods who was driving C Squadron's Recce Officer's armoured car witnessed the aftermath of the Gordon's battle.

'We passed some of 7 RTR's Churchills being back loaded with ominous holes in their turrets – just to cheer us up. ... finally getting up to the tanks later in the day, we witnessed a scene, which remains with me today. C Squadrons Churchills were on the skyline blazing merrily and pouring out dense clouds of black smoke, with their ammunition going off like a firework display. Their de-horsed crews were coming back through the corn, their faces registering the shock of what had just happened to them. The infantry, having been unable to reach [retain] their objective, were returning also and were regrouping prior to digging-in. What a shook us all was the fact that we had been encouraged to believe that our Churchill tanks were practically invincible and the truth was very sobering indeed.'

The Gordons withdrew north across the Sabley stream and dug in astride

Hitlerjungend Panzer Grenadiers pose alongside a kill on 26 June 1944. A few Cromwells reached Tourville but not all returned.

the Cheux to Collville Road. Their casualties for 26 June are difficult to calculate due to the declared 'loss' of the company in Colleville but they are estimated to have been in excess of one hundred. Also in action for the first time, C Squadron left eight of their seventeen Churchills burning on the battlefield. However, only three tank crew were killed, although fifteen men were wounded.

The British attacks petered out as darkness fell. SS-*Hauptsturmführer* Hans Siegle summed up the situation at the end of the tank battle:

> *'The enemy has withdrawn, probably to the southern fringe of Cheux. The breakthrough spot is closed, mission accomplished. It is getting dark.'*

Overnight Siegler was tasked to tow back abandoned 105mm field artillery pieces to positions south of the railway line.

German Counter Attacks

Meanwhile, back in St Manvieu, the remnants of the Scots Fusiliers' and 6 KOSB continued to clear the village. During the afternoon and evening, there were two counter-attacks by *Hitlerjugend's* tanks and infantry, reinforced by the promised Panzer *Kompanie* from 21st Panzer Division. These attacks from the east were largely beaten off by intensive artillery fire. By this stage of the war, the British artillery had developed into a flexible organization, capable of quickly concentrating its massive firepower on a single target, under control of even junior Forward Observation Officers (FOO). However, 6 KOSB, with its companies half dug-in around buildings, paddocks and orchards, was prepared for the counter-attack. Lieutenant Woollcombe recalled:

> *'The village was attacked, and C Company took the strain. Confusion seemed unending. In A Company, we sat tight. Again and again the British guns spoke, as a field regiment rained shells into the dusk for prolonged minutes in a wide protective line. Nobody budged until gradually the whole shapeless action petered out.'*

Having been badly hit by artillery and repulsed by the Scotsmen amongst the ruins of St Manvieu, the German counter-attacks failed as night fell.

Relief in Place by 43 Wessex Division

Also moving on the battlefield as night fell on 26 June were the newly arrived Westcountry infantrymen, belonging to famous regiments such as the Dorsets, Somersets and Wiltshires. Their task was to follow up and take over positions secured by 'the Jocks'; thus releasing 44 and 46 Brigades to move forward to take the northern slopes of the Odon Valley. As EPSOM developed, the Wessex were to expand the corridor to the east.

129 and 214 Brigades had spent most of the day moving up from Bracy, as 15th Scottish and 11th Armoured Divisions vacated the assembly areas and FUPs. 129 Brigade, following up behind 44 (Lowland) Brigade, was first into action. Wiltshireman, Sergeant Regt Romain recalled:

> *'We moved off and the distant sounds of war became nearer and more intense – the lazy howling of the naval shells became cancelled out by the field artillery, both British and German, then the sharp cracks of 25-pounders and 88mm guns, superseded by* Spandau *and* Bren gun *firing as we moved into the battle area. We lost quite a few men to the carpet of mortar bombs that dropped around us and we were becoming excited with that atmosphere of battle.'*

During this move forward, the Wessex infantry had finally abandoned as impractical the bicycles that had been issued, to 'mobile companies' for transport to the battlefield.

As recorded in 4 Wiltshire's (4 Wilts) battalion war diary, its: 'Recce party moved at 1100 hours under the CO to area St Manvieu. A German counter-attack was still in progress on arrival of the battalion's Recce Party in the village. Main body of battalion was ready to move at 1200 hours'. Even thought they were ready to take over from the Scots as planned, 4 Wilts did not in fact move until 2030 hours. One Wiltshireman commented, that 'That day we learnt the first lesson of war; there is an awful lot of waiting around in battle'. Approaching St Manvieu in the pouring rain, it was apparent that fighting was still going on in and around the village. 'They found the village was distinctly not taken.' It was a nightmare relief. Expecting to take over from 6 RSF, the Wiltshiremen found that St Manvieu was mainly held by 6 KOSB, which in the gathering gloom, added to the confusion. The battalion's war diary stated dryly: 'Take over took place in darkness and mortar fire was in progress during take-over'. A member of the Battalion explained that 'Our second lesson was learnt in St Manvieu and that was that no amount of training prepares you for the reality of battle. Fear and confusion makes even the simplest task difficult to achieve.' One factor that confused the Wiltshires was that the 'Jocks were using captured *Spandaus* that, in the dark, with their high rate of fire sounded very different to our slower firing Bren guns'. Another factor was that the tanks were closed down, as their commanders justifiably feared the *Hitlerjugend's* isolated riflemen who shot at any exposed head and shoulders. Consequently, the infantry found it difficult to communicate with the Churchills and to coordinate their activities. The result was 'Total disorganization, as everybody fired at everybody else'. Nevertheless, 4 Wilts had relieved the Jocks by midnight.

Staff officers at 1 SS Panzerkorps Headquarters brief commanders on the dangerous situation on the Odon front.

While 129 Brigade was taking over, SS-*Sturmbannführer* Krause ordered the remnants of I/26 SS Pz Grs around St Manvieu to break out. 1 and 3 *Kompanies* were, however to hold their current positions on the shoulder of the British breakthrough. SS-*Unterscharführer* Heinrich Bassenauer described the withdrawal:

> *'After darkness we assembled for the breakout: in the lead, Papa Krause, a huge figure and a shining fatherly example, followed by the rest of his battalion, including our own wounded and prisoners. Unnoticed, we slipped through the English [sic] in a tall grain field, crossed the Caen – Fontenay Road, and reached the Marcelet – Verson road, where we were welcomed by our own units. During the following day, we moved into new positions at the southern slope of the Carpiquet airfield.'*

Further west 5 Wilts was to take over positions from 8 RS in the le Gaule area. Sergeant Romain described how the battalion moved forward:

> *'From Brecy we travelled through Norrey, then left the road to sweep across country to le Gaule. My first sickening sight of death in the fighting was to see two of the Royal Scots infantrymen straddling the barbed wire fence as we entered the village. ... We hadn't been there long before we were mortared and I dived into the nearest hole. It was a German latrine! I came out quicker than I went in – smelling – and fighting mad.'*

5 Wilts's relief in place at le Gaule, completed at 0300 hours, was the only part of the Wessex Division's first operation that went to plan, all be it well behind schedule.

214 Brigade was to take over defence of Cheux and le Haut du Bosq from 46 (Highland) Brigade. On the main axis, mixed in with 11th Armoured Division and 46 Brigade's transport, 5 Duke of Cornwall's Light Infantry (5 DCLI) and 1 Worcesters spent most of the night in traffic jams that separated the marching infantry from their vehicles and support weapons. 'It was an extremely unpleasant baptism, as we were wet through and being regularly shelled.' wrote a Worcesters officer. The DCLI's historian recorded that:

> *'In such confusion, and in the dark, it was not practicable for the Fifth to take over until daybreak, and in this the Brigade commander concurred. It was a night of heavy rain and the battalion started to move forward at 2 a.m., partly across the field in which a mass of artillery was busily digging in.'*

Because of the confusion, with too many troops using a single axis, with remnants of a determined enemy still active and with heavy mortaring impeding progress, by dawn 214 had failed to relief 46 Brigade.

Summary of the First Day's Operations

A remarkably frank view of the fighting on 26 June 1944 is to be found in VIII Corps's midnight situation report which, is recorded in their war diary:

> *'All units (except 3 RTR) were in action for the first time and the majority of the officers and NCO gained their first battle experience. All reports indicate that the units were well led and that troops fought bravely, skilfully and daringly. They were facing an enemy who fought with fanatical determination, in terrain, which he knew well and had prepared for defence. The broken terrain and inaccurate maps made orientation difficult ... causing first reports to indicate greater progress than had in reality been the case.*
>
> *'The broken terrain was advantageous to the defenders and the enemy made full use of this advantage. The fighting was mostly at short range....*
>
> *'When there were indications of a breakthrough on a narrow front, both flanks were open and the broken ground again helped the enemy. He missed no opportunity to harass our flanks.'*

Once through the enemy's main position, the British were advancing across the grain of the country. For example, with most roads running east – west, the local road running south through Cheux was expected to bear hundreds of wheeled vehicles and with heavy rain, it and other cleared cross country routes were soon reduced to mud. As expected, a narrow salient was beginning to form that eventually became known as the 'Scottish Corridor'. Meanwhile, the Germans still occupied dominating positions on the Rauray Spur. In addition, enemy artillery observers on the high ground at Carpiquet, had good views across EPSOM's lower ground and German commanders had plenty of notice of renewed British attacks.

With enemy anti-tank and dual purpose 88mm guns surviving the bombardment and the *Hitlerjugend's* Mark IVs of II/12 SS Pz Regt redeploying to face 15th Scottish Division, the British armour was fighting its own battle for survival. Consequently, the tanks and infantry were not combining their combat power to best effect. Referring to the first day's fighting, Major General Pip Roberts said that 'Co-operation between 15th Scottish and 11th Armoured was not very close; we rather went our separate ways'.

Even though a degree of tactical surprise was achieved, the Highland and Lowland Brigades were not able to smash their way through 26 SS Pz Gr Regt's defensive positions, as quickly as envisaged. This gave the *Hitlerjugend* an opportunity to regain its balance and its midnight situation report recorded:

> *'While strong enemy tank forces advanced in the area north east of*

2nd Das Reich SS Panzer Division Panthers during their hurried drive east towards the 'Scottish Corridor'.

> *Norrey until 2000 hours, the remains of 12 SS Pi Bn, 26 SS Pz Gr Regt and 12 SS Pz Recce Bn, and in particular 12 SS Pz Regt under SS Obersturmbannführer Wunsch, repelled all enemy attacks. After all these crises had been overcome, a new main line of defence has been formed, with the weak available forces.'*

These 'weak available forces' were supplemented over night by SS panzer grenadiers and pioneers who had been by-passed or had gone to ground during the day and made their way south under cover of darkness.

Despite VIII Corps failing to keep up with its planned rates of advance and the poor armour-infantry coordination, SS-*Obergruppenführer* Dietrich, at HQ I SS *Panzerkorps*, was clamouring for support from Seventh *Armee*,

A halftrack belonging to the pioneer battalion of 12th Hitlerjungend SS Panzer Division during the fighting in June 1944.

fearing an overnight British attack. He signalled:

'If further reinforcements are not sent up to night, a break-through on both sides of Cheux cannot be prevented.'

According to Hubert Meyer:

'The line consisted, especially in the central sector, of a chain of dispersed strongpoints without any depth. It could not withstand a renewed strong attack, in particular of strong tank forces.'

'Panzermeyer', recalled this period:

'Time had lost meaning for us. We worked on a situation map by the glimmer of candlelight and prepared new defensive positions. I waited desperately for reinforcements'.

The *Hitlerjugend's* report continued on similiar lines:

'The Division expects that the enemy will renew his attack on 27.6.44 from Cheux – St Manvieu – Norrey area, despite his high losses, in order to capture Caen. The Division will defend its position using all available forces. Combat ready are: 30 Pz IVs, 17 Panthers, 233 armoured personnel carriers etc and 14 heavy anti-tank guns.'

Of the German reinforcements promised earlier in the day, the two *Leibstandarte* infantry battalions were still stranded at St Germain without fuel and were unlikely to arrive before dawn. However, nearer the front were elements of 2nd and 21st Panzer Divisions. These formations, following Rommel's instruction at 2100 hours, that 'everything which can be assembled must be thrown into the fight', were each to provide a *kampfgruppe* based on a tank battalion. In addition, *Kampfgruppe* Weidinger, the leading element of 2nd *Das Reich* SS Panzer Division was driving east from St Lo. Also moving towards the EPSOM battle area, was another battalion of 7th *Werferbrigade's Nebelwerfers* or multi-barrel rocket mortars.

As the evening and the night passed without a resumption of the British attack, the mood at HQ I SS *Panzerkorps* changed from desperation to optimism. A watchkeeper recorded SS-*Oberstgruppenführer* Dietrich's view in Seventh *Armee's* war diary that the day's fighting 'was a complete defensive success'. Shortly afterwards a further message recorded that Dietrich intended to mount a counter-attack based on the eighty panzers available or on the way to the battlefront. The scene was set for the largest set piece battle since D-Day to continue.

As a final note, Major Joscelyne's words in A Squadron, 7 RTR's war diary, summarize the impact of the day's fighting on British units:

'That day we lost five tanks knocked out and three on mines. We became a squadron of ten tanks and wiser and more sober men. We had lost some of our best officers, NCOs and men, in a few hours, after years of intensive training.'

CHAPTER FOUR

Day 2 – Capture of the Odon Bridges

While SS-*Obergruppenführer* Dietrich was optimistically planning a counter-attack to round off his 'defensive victory', Lieutenant General Sir Richard O'Connor was planing to renew battle at dawn on 27 June 1944. Headquarters 15th Scottish Division had issued the following radio orders, at 2300 hours the previous evening:

> *'Enemy now reduced to last reserves on our front. Essential to secure crossings over R ODON as early as possible tomorrow 27 Jun. 227 Bde will secure GRAINVILLE SUR ODON, with 10 HLI attacking first light, with arty and tk sp as already arranged. 227 Bde will thereafter, push down to secure crossings north of GAVRUS 915623 and at 930630* [Toumauville] *as quickly as possible supported by two regts 29 Armd Bde. 44 Bde on relief by 129 Bde will conc ... in Div Res. 46 Bde*

Soldiers of 227 Brigade shaking out into formation in their FUP.

on relief will take over COLLEVEILLE from 227 Bde and exploit towards MOUEN.'

The immediate objective was the capture of the Odon crossings by 15th Scottish Division. VIII Corps's subsequent objective, to be taken by 11th Armoured Division, remained the River Orne and the open country beyond. West of VIII Corps's boundary, 49th West Riding Division was to continue its attempt to clear the Rauray Spur, which uncaptured had done so much to undermine the previous day's attack.

The plan was to continue with EPSOM, making only minor adjustments. To do anything else would have been impossible as, in the confusion of battle, it had taken most of the night to gain an accurate picture of exactly where units were, their strength and where the enemy were. Overnight, the divisional logistic units struggled forward through mud, rubble and traffic chaos with combat supplies. However, with the short June nights, many resupply vehicles were still forward at dawn and added to the difficulties, as the fighting echelons started moving again.

Major General 'Pip' Roberts, having seen his tanks stopped in their tracks the previous afternoon, was to wait for 15th Division to bludgeon its way through the enemy positions before unleashing his tanks again. However, with no less than five brigades of infantry and three brigades of armour crammed into about four square miles, it would be difficult for the attackers to gather momentum before they struck the enemy.

Rauray

Before dawn, the Hallamshire Battalion advanced and established positions at the southern end of Tessel Wood, while 11 DLI held positions gained the previous evening. Advancing between these two salients 4 Lincoln and the Tyne Scots cleared the central area around la Grande Ferme. Now less exposed, 11 DLI advanced at midday to attack and eventually capture Rauray. However, dominating positions on the ridge further south including Grainville, were still in German hands.

49th West Riding Division

227 Highland Brigade's renewed Attack

227 Highland Brigade's plan to renew their advance is recorded in an entry in their war diary.

> '10 HLI will attack to the west of Cheux together with tanks of 31st Tank Brigade. They will capture the Odon crossing near Gavrus. H - Hour at 0445 hours.

> '2 A & S H [Argyll and Sutherland Highlanders] will attack east of Cheux, with tanks as previously scheduled, and will take the crossing south of Tourville [Toumauville Bridge]. H-Hour at 0530 hours.

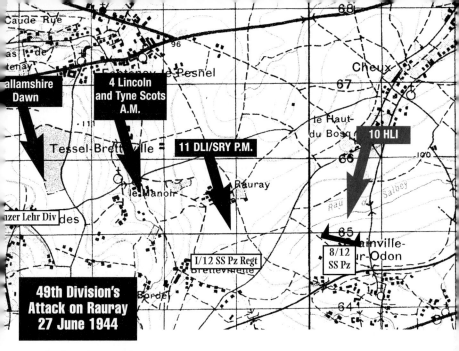

Map labels:
Caude Rue
as l de
tenay
allamshire Dawn
4 Lincoln and Tyne Scots A.M.
96
e Pesnel
Cheux
67
le Haut-du Bos
10 HLI
Tessel-Brettville
11 DLI/SRY P.M.
100
Rauray
Salbey
azer Lehr Div des
le Manoir
Rau
65
nville-r-Odon
I/12 SS Pz Regt
8/12 SS Pz
brettevuene
49th Division's Attack on Rauray 27 June 1944
Bordel
64

[Delayed to 0730].

'29 Armoured Brigade will be prepared to follow up success by 227 Brigade and 159 Infantry Brigade [11th Armoured] will advance via the Odon crossings and establish bridgeheads, as soon as the first tank units have crossed the R. Odon.'

10 HLI was the first unit of 227 Brigade to renew the attack shortly after dawn on 27 June. Lieutenant Robert Sherrin was not impressed:

'...when we were ordered in again my heart sank. I'd seen so many lads go down, that I saw no chance whatever of success and it all seemed absolutely pointless. I thought, Christ, we've got so much artillery why not blast them to hell? It was sheer suicide to send men into an attack against prepared positions and frontally.'

Despite a heavy preliminary bombardment, SS-*Hauptsturmführer* Hans Siegel's 8 *Kompanie* II/12 Pz Regt, still with only four serviceable Mark IVs, was ready and waiting. However, now they were supported by remnants from II/26 SS Pz Gr and 12 SS Pi Battalion. Siegel, writing in the third person, describes how he was away on a recce when the British bombardment started and, in his absence, the panzers pulled back:

'The panzers are ordered back into their starting positions. They arrive just in time as an infantry attack begins from the heights south of Cheux, accompanied by tanks, which are, however, still holding back.

'They let the attack approach them frontally. Fire only from machine guns, not from the panzer guns, so as not to betray the presence of *panzers prematurely. Open fire only on the commander's [Siegel's] order. We let them come close and then hammer, at short distance, concentrated fire from four machine guns at the massed attackers who are anxiously firing bullets into the terrain, without aiming. Experience has shown that this tactic works, and the result here is that they run back in panic, under the salvos from our machine guns. We open fire from our panzer guns only on the tanks attacking with the second wave. Again, we achieved full success, without losses of our own. The enemy crews bail out in panic from burning and exploding tanks. The rest of them turn away and, with them, the infantry who disappear behind the hills.'*

The Scot's divisional historian wrote that:

> *'By 8.30 AM 10 HLI were again held up... All day the HLI remained pinned under intense mortar-fire. Casualties were heavy, and no praise can be too great for the work of the stretcher-bearers.'*

The four valiant but ill-fated attacks by 10 HLI on the second day of EPSOM, however, served to fix the enemy's attention immediately south of

The area south of le Haut du Bosq that 10 HLI tried to clear.

The area south of le Haut du Bosq where 10 HLI were halted by Seigel on the evening of 26 and agian on the morning of 27 July 1944.

Cheux

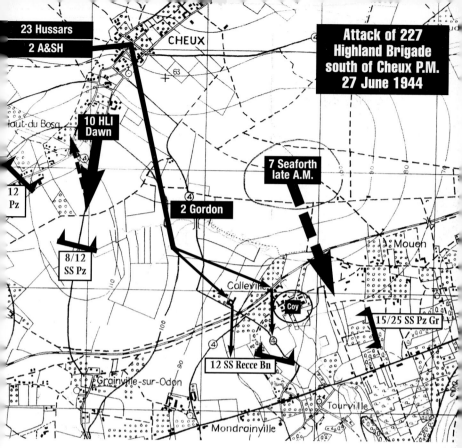

laut-du Bosq

10 HLI Dawn

7 Seaforth late A.M.

12 Pz

2 Gordon

Mouen

8/12 SS Pz

Colleville

Coy

15/25 SS Pz Gr

12 SS Recce Bn

Grainville-sur-Odon

Tourville

Mondrainville

Cheux. Thus thinning the German line elsewhere.

The HLI's CO was not a happy man. After the battle, he gathered his officers and senior NCOs together to address them. According to Sergeant Len Graves the CO stood on an ammunition box and said:

'I am very disappointed with you all. You've shown me what you're made of; you're yellow, practically the whole bloody lot of you! I am ashamed of you. There will be some changes made and they won't be very nice, I can tell you. I've never seen such a bloody awful performance, it really was stinking.'

'We looked at each other and some blokes began muttering about what a fine example he was. One sergeant near me said, "If he thinks it's f.....g well easy why the f..k doesn't he get out and do it his bloody self?" I can tell you we all felt the same and our opinion of him went right down, we didn't care a shit for him, with our pals lying out their dead and maimed while he stood there!'

Former Sergeant Major Bransen candidly spoke about the aftermath of the CO's address:

97

'I was made sergeant in late 1940 after seeing no action at all and spent the war in Britain, ending up with the HLI. I soon learnt in Normandy – too late – that I was not really cut out for it at all. I was not really the combat type and was happier in admin. But I had no choice but to try and set an example. When the shooting started I was terrified and flunked it: I just fell down in a faint and like the rest, ran back the way I'd come. After the CO gave us the bollocking the RSM took me outside with two more Senior NCOs and said "You men are hereby reduced to the ranks, you're privates from now on. Get out of my bloody sight".'

This type of incident was played out throughout the army, as men buckled under the searching rigours of combat, be they in action for the first time or in action on one occasion too many.

Nonetheless, 10 HLI in fixing the enemy's attention had created opportunity for 2 A&SH, whose CO, Lieutenant Colonel Tweedie, was summoned to HQ 227 Brigade. He received his orders at 0530 hours. Supported by 23 Hussars (23 H), his battalion was to advance through 2 Gordons and seize the Tourmauville Bridge across the Odon. His H-Hour was to be 0730 hours. 'Weary waiting north of Cheux gave place to a mad scramble – such is war. It says a lot for their battle procedure that the Argyles got off on time.' With a start line north of Cheux, the battalion's

Morning 27 June 23rd Hussars follow 2 A&SH of 227 Brigade towards Colleville.

first problem was to get through the chaotic choke-point around the village. Having forced their way through, they passed through 2 Gordons and advanced towards Colleville. By taking this route, the Argyles avoided the exposed Ring Contour 100. Colonel Tweedie also ignored his open flanks and the battle between 10 HLI and Siegel's panzers, a thousand yards to the west. Corporal Campbell was in charge of one of the Argyle's 6-pounder anti-tank guns covering the move through Cheux:

'Suddenly 100 yards away a tank appeared side-on in a gateway; this was my first German. He hadn't seen us and fired at something else. We fired one of the brand new 6-pounder discarding sabot rounds into its side. With the first shot nothing seemed to happen, so I grabbed a second and saw a spurt of flame come out from between the bogey wheels. Then I saw a bloke jumping from the turret – he was well alight. We fired a third shot and the whole thing blew up, knocking me over.'

The Argyles pressed on and the battalion reached the railway line, entered Colleville and 'mopped it up after house to house fighting'. SS-*Sturmbannführer* Hubert Meyer, however, typically complained that 2 A&SH had:

'... encountered a particularly weak spot in our defences. Only weak guards of the Recce Battalion, which had been moved from the operations area Rauray during the night in order to close a dangerous gap here as best they could, were located north of Colleville. The command post of the Battalion was in Mondrainville. 1 Battery of Flakregiment 53, *part* Flaksturmregiment *was also there. Other than that, only members of supply units and stragglers had prepared the town for defence.'*

However, this German force had anti-tank punch with 88mm flak guns in the ground defence role and a clear force multipliers in the form of stout stone buildings for the infantry to fight from. The resulting fighting in Colleville was a protracted affair that went on well into the afternoon.

SS-*Oberscharführer* August Zinssmeister, an armoured car commander in 12 SS Recce Battalion, wrote:

'Dead and wounded Tommies are lying at the railway crossing. They are members of an assault squad caught by artillery fire. A heavy artillery barrage is raining on Mondrainville and our sector again. The whole area is full of smoke.

'We encounter a section of our riflemen withdrawing along our path from the railway. A counter-attack with panzers and motorcycle riflemen fails and Tommy is able to get into the village to our flank. We

fire everything we have, at close range, with devastating effect. The Tommies send up flares and hammer us with heavy shells.

'We are reinforced and return for another counter attack along the northern edge of the town. The bushes and hedges are full of English infantry and the firefight continues without pause. The English infantry manage to advance further and now we are coming under anti-tank fire. I order let's go and we run into a Sherman and I look into its muzzle!'

The SS had been forced out of Colleville and 15th Scottish had finally secured a foothold in the close country on the northern edge of the Odon Valley.

Cheux and the German Counter-Attacks

As has already been described, overnight 44 Brigade had been relieved in St Manvieu and le Gaule to become divisional reserve in the area of Le Mensil Patry. However, 214 Brigade had been unable to relieve 46 Highland Brigade in Cheux and le Haut du Bosq, thus preventing 46 Brigade, less 7 Seaforth, from being available for other tasks on the morning of 27 June.

However, at 0200 hours, 5 Duke of Cornwall's Light Infantry (5 DCLI) started to move forward to take over from the Cameronians who were in the northern part of le Haut du Bosq. In the southern part of the hamlet, 10 HLI had taken up position following their failure to take Grainville the previous evening.

Major George Taylor. Afterwards CO 5 DCLI.

Major George Taylor, Second in Command of 1 Worcester, recalled that as Lieutenant Colonel Atherton led his battalion past, 'I wished him luck. He replied sombrely: "I'll need it George".' Private Denis Coulsen recalled 5 DCLI's advance from the FUP:

'We formed up. It was not a bad morning but we were still wet from the soaking we got during the night. We'd had some breakfast but hardly felt like eating. Our battalion was crouched down and ready to go; we had some Churchills of the 7th Tanks. Then the whistles blew and off we went down a grassy slope and in no time, we began to get fire from two sides and we were pinned down. Our officer was hit at once and we heard no more from him. Our Sergeant tried to get us moving but as soon as he rose up he was hit in the arm and fell down moaning. We lay there quite unable to move; the bullets and shells were whizzing overhead and into the ground about

Infantry and supporting Churchills advancing through the waist high corn.

us and some more men were hit. Then there were shells falling among us and some panic came so that first a few and then the lot of us were forced to run back the way we came. I had my head down and I could only see one of my mates and not many others of the 500 or so men who started out, but amazingly most of them got back sooner or later. As we crashed down again among the bushes and broken trees I saw our Colonel standing with his glasses by his scout car, and his face was a picture, a mix of anguish and fury.'

Also withdrawing was Private John Tilsen who explained:

'I ran back in a hell of a sweat just behind Denis with all that stuff flying about us and was very surprised that we were in one piece. Yes, I saw our Colonel watching, and even before we'd got our breath back the reserve company was sent rushing forward down that hill, past the knocked out Churchills, and they went rushing down the slope waving white sheets and Red Cross armbands to get to the wounded, and some were hit. It was awful to see and I just buried my face in my arm. I'd seen enough and I cried. We'd had a bad introduction to battle – no mistake.'

It took all of Lieutenant Colonel Atherton's leadership to get the shocked men moving forward to le Haut du Bosq behind the reserve companies who were now leading. They were being engaged from the Rauray Spur, to the DCLI's right, which was not finally captured until later in the day. But, after a shaky start, the men who became one of the most effective Allied infantry battalions fighting in North West Europe, soon had an opportunity to show their true qualities.

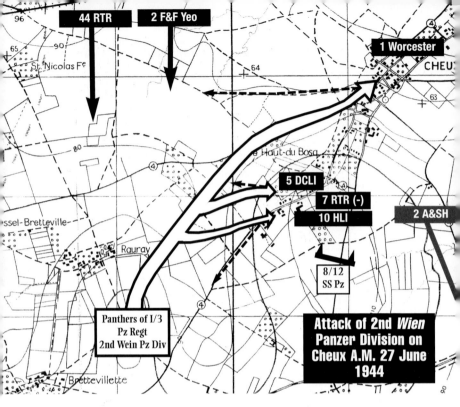

Reaching le Haut du Bosq, 5 DCLI found that the company of 9 Cameronians and their anti-tank guns, who they were to relieve, had already vacated their positions. To the Cornwall's consternation, le Haut du Bosq was back in hands of enemy riflemen. According to the regimental history:

> 'This unfortunate misunderstanding complicated matters for the Fifth, but they started to dig in amongst the orchards and at the same time carried out an active hunt for the snipers who abounded, many of them young SS fanatics who neither gave or received quarter. The chaos of battle was everywhere in evidence. Not far from the village to the north west could be seen part of 11th Armoured Division [44RTR and 2 F&F Yeo], their tanks grouping for action under a steady bombardment from the enemy artillery. On the other side of the village, some flame-thrower tanks were flushing the hedgerows for snipers. In front the crackle of small arms fire never ceased and periodically parties of wounded men and prisoners under escort made their way to the rear.'

As far as the Cornwalls were concerned, they were not in the front line but were to hold le Haut du Bosq in case the troops fighting in front of them were driven back by a counter-attack. Captain Jobson and Corporal Rohan were returning to D Company HQ following a successful 'sniper' hunt in the surrounding farm buildings, when:

> 'About ten yards up the road we were surprised and glad to see six
> nice big tanks trundle up the road and turn into Company
> Headquarters' Orchard. "Always nice to have armour in support –
> pretty decent guns on them – funny camouflage. My God! German
> crosses on their turrets!" This last observation was too awful to be
> ignored and violent evasive action was taken by the two of us,'

The arrival of six Panther tanks in the centre of a battalion position with out
a shot being fired, on that battalion's first day in action was a dangerous
event. What had gone wrong and would a shaky battalion break and run?

Plenty had gone wrong, particularly for the Germans. Their normally
smooth regrouping procedures had broken down under the pressure of the
British attack. The *Kampfgruppe* sent from 2nd *Wien* Panzer Division in
response to Rommel's demands the previous evening, proved to be a
battalion of Panthers (I/3 Pz Regt), without infantry. Initially, the battalion
reported to Panzer *Lehr's* Divisional Headquarters, which had contained
49th Division in its sector, and consequently dispatched the Panthers east
to support the *Hitlerjugend*. SS-*Sturmbannführer* Meyer complained that I/3
Pz Regt had not reported to his headquarters and said:

> '... this attack was an obvious mistake. In this situation, not even a
> panzer battalion accompanied by infantry in battalion strength could
> have achieved lasting success. The enemy superiority was much too
> great. Instead, the Panthers could have extraordinarily contributed,
> from favourable positions, in the defence against the attack from Cheux.
> This is a case where despite best intentions, wrong actions had been
> ordered in ignorance of the real situation and local conditions. One of
> the reasons why the divisional command staff had remained in Verson
> was to be able to direct operations close to the quickly changing
> circumstances.'

At 0930 hours, the Panthers advanced from Rauray north east to Cheux.
Some were engaged by 7 RTR, supporting the stalled 10 HLI, who claimed
two kills. 10 HLI's war diary record that, on their western flank, at:

> '1000 hrs tanks [a part of I/3 Pz Regt] broke through into battalion
> area and were engaged by own anti-tank guns. Five enemy tanks were
> knocked out. Remainder withdrew and the position was restored by
> 1100 hrs. One signal truck burnt out after receiving direct hit.'

However, most of the Panthers bypassed the HLI and pressed on, with a
reinforced platoon, advancing via a sunken road into le Haut du Bosq,
while the main body continued towards Cheux. The six panzers heading
for 5 DCLI drove past B Company's position without being engaged.
Captain Jobson continued his account:

> 'The leading tank went on for fifty yards, and knocked out a whole

troop of 17-pounder anti-tank guns just coming up.

'Cpl Rohan and myself found ourselves in Sergeant Hicks's mortar pit. After a brief pow-wow, it was decided that Sergeant Hicks, with his PIAT, should start shooting up the tanks from the back. I went off and organised the three PIAT teams from the three platoons. On returning, I had the pleasure of watching Major Fry and Ptes Jeffries and Parrish being chased all around the orchard. Each time a tank moved it was necessary for them to move also. Funny to watch but not for them. The rest of the Company Headquarters were in their slits, with the tanks actually on top or around them. Next, two German dispatch riders came down the road and Major Fry and I had the honour and pleasure of killing the first Germans in the battalion area. The German tanks then started to edge forward and knocked out the two 6-pounder guns in D Company's area, wounding most of the crew. Battalion HQ was their next objective. It was a nice hull down shoot for them at about fifty yards range. Very soon there were soft vehicles and carriers brewing up and much activity was near the Battalion HQ ditch. Our 6-pounders replied despite the fact that they were under direct fire. Lieutenant Colonel Atherton was killed in a gallant attempt to keep one gun firing. He was acting as loader, as the rest of the crew was knocked out. At this time, I met the IO.

'We lay in a shallow ditch in an orchard under the barrel of a 75mm

le Haut du Bosq where the Wessex Division's 17-pounder guns were knocked out.

Cheux
Church

10 HLI and Siegel's
Kompanie

Sergeant Frank Grigg's photographs of the Panthers in the orchard at Cheux knocked out by 5 DCLI.

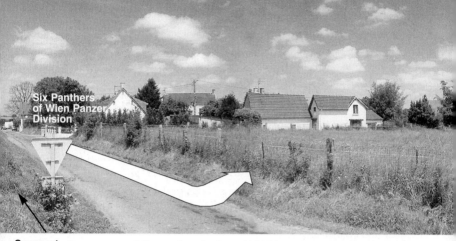

Six Panthers of Wien Panzer Division

Sergeant Grigg's Trench

Panorama of the orchard where DCLI knocked out five Panthers.

gun with the tracks of the tank not two feet from us. Prayers were said amongst other things! Four PIATs were hitting the tanks up their backside and the Germans did not like it. One fled, hit three times by a 17 Platoon PIAT. ...he got away badly hit and the crew well shaken. Sergeant Hicks knocked out another one at short range. Two more went round the corner and were worried by Captain Blackwell of C Company who led a PIAT party. He knocked one out and the other turned itself over in its excitement to escape. Sergeant Willison's 6-pounder accounted for another when to his own surprise, and everyone else's, the Panther brewed up at 100 yards range.

'The hunting of the crews was the next phase and exciting sport it made. Four prisoners were captured and about nine Germans were killed.'

Having knocked out five Panthers in close quarter battle, 5 DCLI, a Territorial Army battalion, in action for the first time, with a shaky start two hours earlier, was now the talk of VIII Corps.

While the Cornwalls were in action at le Haut du Bosq, 1 Worcester was taking over the defence of Cheux from 2 Glasgow Highlanders.

'Not a building was whole and most of them were knocked to pieces. The narrow roads were littered with equipment of all sorts including wreckage of our trucks and tanks, some still burning.'

However, with the Royal Artillery's 17-pounders still in place, I/3 Pz Regt's Panthers were unable to press home their attack in Cheux.

The Worcester's companies had deployed into positions on the outskirts of the village to avoid the worst of the enemy shelling. As a fresh battalion, they found that there were too few slit trenches for them to occupy, so heavy had been the Highlander's casualties in Cheux. Having taken over the defence of the village, Major Riddle held a Company Orders

Cheux

Orchard

5 DCLI's
Bn Headquarters

Group to co-ordinate the details of the defence and while doing so, a mortar bomb killed him and his four officers. Mortar bombs were not the only problem in Cheux. Almost twenty-four hours after the initial occupation individuals were still being shot by 'snipers' hiding in the ruins. Once the Battalion was in position, the Worcester's Sniper Section was sent into the village, where these masters of field craft, observation and marksmanship ruthlessly hunted down the *Hitlerjugend*. The Germans were in fact not trained snipers at all but where what Brigadier Carver later insisted his Brigade referred to as 'isolated riflemen', who bravely fought on. No match for the handful of British marksmen most of the *Hitlerjugend* still hiding in Cheux, died from a single shot to the head or upper chest. With the final clearance of the enemy from the village, the order was gradually imposed on this battlefield choke point.

Cheux Church.

On outskirts of the village, the hedgerows still harboured young, determined SS troopers who were also prepared to die. 1 Worcester's historian recorded an incident that demonstrated the fanaticism of the *Hitlerjugend* and the typical response they engendered.

> '*On one occasion a German soldier was seen coming cautiously towards a platoon locality with his hands up above his head, but when he got close he suddenly threw a grenade, which luckily did not do any damage, and the only looser was the man himself, who was immediately shot. This soon got around and from then on, no one had the slightest compassion for the other side. Few or no prisoners were taken.*'

Without a sniper section to counter the enemy shooting, 151 (Ayrshire Yeomanry) Field Regiment RA's field newspaper *The Yeoman* recorded:

> '*The tenacity of snipers was well demonstrated by the fact that two Boche were found in woods in the centre of the gun area 24 and 48 hours respectively after we entered the area. One of the above men who gave himself up to 125 Battery had remained hidden in the woods with a wound to his left leg. He belonged to the Engineer Battalion of 12 SS Pz Division. He was obviously frightened that he was going to be shot.*'

South east of Cheux, 7 Seaforth, which had been unable to secure the crest of Ring Contour 100 the previous evening, cleared the feature at 1000 hours, having found that the enemy, outflanked by the Argyles, had withdrawn. In due course, the Seaforth took over positions previously occupied by 2 Gordons, who had followed the Argyles into Colleville.

One of the anti-tank regiments' 17-pounders that had just knocked out a Panther tank that belonged to 2nd Wien Panzer Division on the outskirts of Cheux.

However, on the ridge resolute defenders from SS-*Hauptsturmführer* Siegel's 8 *Kompanie* received freshly repaired Mark IVs that maintained their strength, despite the inevitable losses suffered in a protracted battle. Siegel, himself, was badly burnt when his panzer was hit around midday but his *Kompanie* held its positions until later in the afternoon.

Despite his success, Siegel's small force of panzers could not hold the whole front. Further east, 29 Armoured Brigade followed the infantry into Colleville, from where elements of the Brigade were able to advance south behind the Highlanders. At 0925 hours, 11th Armoured Division's war diary recorded that the 'Speed of advance increased, with 29 Armoured Brigade pushing on and 3 RTR going wide towards Mouen'. At this point 101 *Schwere* Panzer Battalion's Tigers intervened. One *kompanie* engaged Shermans advancing across Ring Contour 100 towards their positions in the orchards around Mouen, while a second *kompanie* deployed on the Rauray spur to the west of Seigle's position. However, faced with tanks from no less than one tank and two armoured brigades even the mighty Tigers were overwhelmed. A couple of entries from 11th Armoured Division's war diary give a flavour of the fighting :

'1050 *3 RTR destroy one Tiger at 933658* [Mouen] *and 942670* [Bas de Mouen]. *23 H destroys one Tiger and one 88mm gun and silence further guns* [south of Colleville].

'1055 *owing to the fact that Right of 2 F&F Yeo is being threatened by Tigers from area 900656* [Rauray Spur], *44 RTR* [from 4

A wrecked Panther knocked out by the 17-pounder, pictured opposite.

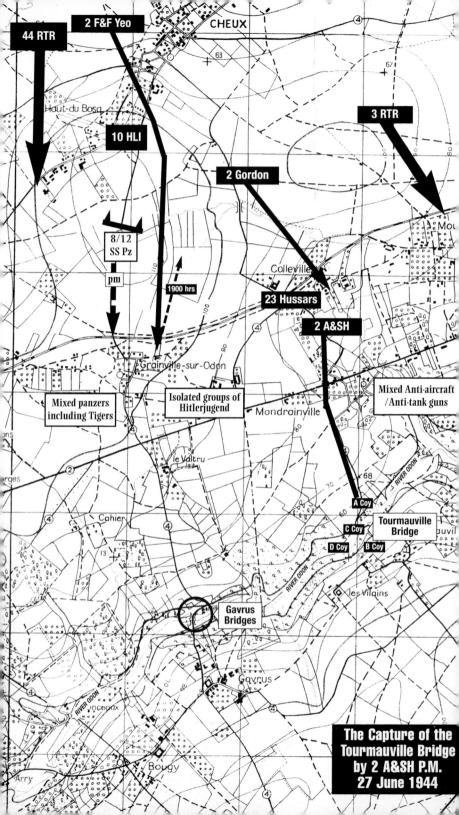

The Capture of the
Tourmauville Bridge
by 2 A&SH P.M.
27 June 1944

Armoured Brigade] *are ordered to move up and protect flank of 2 FF*
Yeo advancing south with them.'

By 1130 hours, the advance was continuing towards the Caen – Villers Bocage Road. Both 227 and 29 Armoured Brigades claim the advance as their success. However, although co-ordination of the two brigade's efforts was virtually impossible, they had a common aim and, more by accident than design, they effectively supported each other. 23 H following 2 A&SH through Colleville, made the most progress but at 1710 hours, '2 F&F Yeo [on the right flank] reported that they expect to reach Grainville shortly'. However, as recorded in 2 FF Yeo's war diary, this was not to be a breakthrough, as:

> *'The German thrust was continuous from the right all day and though A Squadron pushed on to the high ground N of Grainville, the close country on our immediate right, was never cleared'*

At 1910 hours, the news that '2 F&F Yeo report that they are in Grainville and approaching the main road Caen – Villers Bocage' was being passed up the chain of command. This good news was followed by word that they were unable to get across the road due to fire from their right flank and ahead of them. 2230 hours, 2 F&F Yeo were pulling back as darkness fell.

A traffic jam on route. Many logistic vehicles and towed anti-tank guns are protected by a pair of anti-aircraft tanks.

British tanks did not fight at night and habitually withdrew to a leaguer some distance to the rear. The day's fighting had cost 29 Armoured Brigade nineteen ordinary Shermans and five 17-pounder Fireflies while 10 HLI, on the right flank, had lost a further 112 men; almost the equivalent of another whole company.

Capture of the Tourmauville Bridge

The Argyles and 23 H had taken a considerable time to fight through Colleville but by 1500 hours, seven hours after crossing their start line north of Cheux, they had reached the twin villages of Tourville and Mondrainville. These villages, standing on the Caen–Villers-Bocage Road, were covered by patrols from 12 SS Recce Battalion. The 15th's historian wrote that opposition was 'quickly mopped up, after driving off armoured cars which were patrolling the highway and knocking-out one of the two panzers that tried to intervene from eastward.' These panzers summoned to help the recce troops, could not, without infantry support, hope to block the Argyles.

With two companies forming a firm base, 2 A&SH did not dally in the villages. Ignoring the fact that they were in danger of being cut-off Colonel Tweedie ordered an advanced into the Odon Valley. The divisional historian recorded that:

> '... the further advance by B and C Companies, covered by D Company, down the road to Tourmauville for another 1200 yards or so beyond the highway, culminated in the assault by C Company, led by Major Fyfe, to seize the Odon Bridge itself. The whole affair was a

The Caen–Villers-Bocage Road reached by 2 A&SH on the afternoon of 27 June.

Caen

N175

Road leading to the bridge.

The road from the Tourmauville Bridge to Baron. Hill 112 lies almost directly beyond. 23rd Hussars initial thrust up this road was halted, forceing them to take a longer route to the east.

Baron

23 Hussars

Tourmauville Bridge.

tactical masterpiece. About 5 p.m. C Company took the [largely undefended] *bridge intact.'*

Supporting C Company's advance down into the valley was Corporal Campbell and his 6-pounder:

> 'We came under machine gun fire. We unlimbered the gun and traced where we reckoned it was coming from; a house 3-400 yards away. This time we loaded with solid shot and we put a round through the top window and a round through a bottom window. End of machine gun fire! Then C Company charged down across open ground to the bridge. We limbered-up and went down to join the company commander.
>
> 'I went across the bridge and with Major Fyfe went up the road towards Tourmauville. Reaching the open ground, he said "This is as far as we go". I positioned the Company's PIATs and brought the gun up.'

Lieutenant Colonel Tweedie sent both B and D companies across the Tourmauville Bridge to join C Company. Moving up the slope to where there were better fields of fire, the three companies formed a tight bridgehead about two hundred yards in diameter. A Company, which had hither too been in reserve, held the bridge itself and covered the steep approaches to the bridge down which they had just come. Commanders went around their positions coordinating up arcs of fire and started their men digging-in, before the *Hitlerjugend* could counter-attack. Meanwhile, signallers were fighting for radio communications. Deep in a narrow, wooded valley it needed all their skill to get the vital message out that 'QUAGS' (the code word for Tourmauville Bridge) had been taken.

During the evening, Colonel Tweedie sent two strong fighting patrols to the Gavrus Bridges, which were successfully occupied and the patrols radioed Battalion HQ with details of their success. In seizing the Odon Bridges, 2 A&SH has effectively completed, a day late, 15th Scottish Division's original Operation EPSOM mission.

11th Armoured Division Reinforces the Bridgehead

Following behind the Argyles were the 23 Hussars Battlegroup, which included companies of 8 Rifle Brigade (8 RB) mounted in half-tracks. Heading south down the slope to the Odon, the tanks did not like the look of the 'difficult' or close terrain south of the Caen-Villers Bocage road. Consequently, Major Mackenzie's H Company, 8 RB was ordered to debus and move ahead of the tanks towards the bridge. They 'shot up' remaining anti-tank guns and cleared away small groups of *Hitlerjugend* who, armed with *Panzerfausts* were a considerable threat to the tanks.

Half an hour after the Argyles reached the Tourmauville Bridge, H

Signallers of the Hitlerjugend appear to be listening to the sound of aircraft overhead – which would have been Allied.

Company leading the Shermans of C Squadron, 23 Hussars, joined them. According to Corporal Campbell of the Argyles, who was only too aware how exposed his position was:

> *'They were a wonderful sight to see; those tanks coming down the hill. There were cheers all around.'*

Crossing the bridge, as described in 23 H's regimental history, the tanks:

> *'... ground along in low gear up a steep and twisting track through wooded and difficult country until they came out just south of the village of Tourmauville [south of the Odon], where, for the first time, they were able to fan out on ground that gave a good field of fire. Commanders and gunners strained their dust filled eyes. Were some of those bushes camouflaged tanks? One German experienced what was probably the greatest shock of his life. He appeared in a small civilian car from the direction of Esquay. Lance Corporal Evans put an armour piercing shot through the car at a range of twenty yards. Surprisingly the driver managed to get out and, though pursued by Corporal Hoggins with a Sten gun, he got away and was last seen going very fast*

A Sherman belonging to 4th Armoured Brigade and infantry advance through an area, as advertised by the sign, cleared of mines by 279 Field Company RE.

in the direction of Esquay. This was followed almost at once by a short engagement with some guns and infantry in the area of Gavrus'

Although 23 H's leading company/squadron group had found a way down to the Tourmauville Bridge, the route was not fully clear of anti-tank guns that could engage the following squadrons. The Hussar's regimental historian recorded with his usual understatement that:

A Panther knocked out on the Tourville road.

A British tank crew man from 29 Armoured Brigade inspects a knocked-out 88mm gun.

'Even now, the journey through Mondrainville was not without its excitements. The road was not clear. Beside the tanks of B Squadron, which had been damaged or ditched, a Panther had been knocked out and lay with its long barrel stretching across the road. The result was a good deal of congestion. Two Honey tanks were hit and added to the mounting list of derelicts. ... The CO's tank itself had been taken on as a target by the German gunners, as it came through Mondrainville and to those listening on the Forward Link were amused to hear the Colonel come up on the air in the middle of the battle saying. "Get behind me, Sixteen Charlie, there's some bastard shooting me up the dock!"'

By 1925 hours, both the depleted B and C Squadrons were across the bridge, having 'by devious routes made our way down to the river'.

Following up, and trying to make their way through the rubble of Cheux and traffic jams of logistic vehicles, was 11th Armoured Division's 159 Infantry Brigade.

'At 2000 hours, accurate information was scarce. Had we taken the bridge? Where were the enemy? No one knew anything for sure, except that 159 Brigade had orders to cross the Odon before dusk.'

The commander, Brigadier Sandie, did not react well to the pressure of the situation and in 'a chaotic orders group' gave what his battalion commanders considered an unreasonable H-Hour for the advance. The tired and protesting commanding officers were ordered to be at the start line by 2130 hours. 'An order is an order! Carry it out or take the consequences! Into battle!' Major General Roberts was not impressed and the following morning, replaced Brigadier Sandie with Colonel Churcher of the Herefords. However, a VIII Corps staff officer wrote:

> *'It is always desirable when a unit goes into battle for the first time for it to be introduced in such a way that the resultant shock is minimized as far as possible and there is time for a reasonably gradual adjustment to war conditions. ...159 Infantry Brigade was, however, not so lucky in its battle inoculation, for with darkness falling, it had the unenviable task of enlarging the hard won bridgehead during the night, under constant harassing fire from enemy artillery and mortars, and conscious that by daybreak the position must be consolidated against attack so that the armour would have a firm base from which to operate on the morrow.'*

In the gathering darkness, after a chaotic assembly, the leading battalions, 1 Hereford on the right and the 4 King's Shropshire Light Infantry (KSLI)

A Sherman of 44 RTR being refuelled during Operation EPSOM, prior to returning to action.

British infantry taking cover alongside a knocked out Tiger belonging to 101 SS Panzer Battalion at Rauray.

on the left, both managed to cross the Odon. In reserve, 3 Monmouths (3 Mons) were tasked to take up a defensive position on the north bank as brigade reserve.

Major Ned Thornburn's description of 4 KSLI's advance to the Odon portrays the kind of problems the Brigade encountered:

'We set out along this forest avenue at full light infantry pace, interspersed with stretches at the double. I ran from one platoon commander to the next explaining what the plan for the attack was. Mine was the second or third company in the order of march, so at least I didn't have the responsibility of trying to achieve the impossible task of reaching the main [Caen – Villers-Bocage] road. I think we assumed that the enemy would be too alarmed by our numbers to show themselves (how naïve one can be!). By 2115, I knew we had missed the artillery barrage ... I got my two leading platoons lying down along the edge of the forest... I gave the word to commence the attack and we crossed the road. "Time spent in reconnaissance is never wasted", the book says, but of course no one had done any reconnaissance on this start line and when we attempted to charge forward we found the thickest thorn hedge any of us had ever seen in our lives – utterly and

completely unappeasable. I ran along the road for 100 yards or so until I found a gate, and we all walked through it very politely! Little did I think that D Company would deliver its first attack in single file with the company commander leading and reading his map! ...we walked safely straight down to the river where, believe it or not we found straight in front of us an ornamental bridge ...and we walked 400 yards up a steepish pathway to find ourselves at the gates of the Chateau de Baron. We were on our objective without a single casualty and there was not a soul to be seen anywhere. It was about 2245.'

The remainder of the Battalion followed on twenty minutes later.

The Herefords had less difficulty by simply following the road down to the Tourmauville Bridge and deployed beyond 2 A&SH at 2355 hours. Following behind was 3 Monmouths. However, moving across country from the Cheux area, in the dark, the Monmouths veered to far to the east and entered Mouen. Here they left C Company who took up positions in the houses and farm buildings. This isolated company was to play a significant roll during the following morning's fighting. The remainder of the battalion moved down into the Odon Valley and dug in position on the north bank of the river.

By dawn, the bridgehead was firmly held by the infantry, supported by two of 29 Armoured Brigade's regiments. An excellent platform for exploitation had been formed, from which 11th Armoured Division's tanks should be able to advance to the Orne. An entry in C in C West's war diary on the evening of 27 June timed 2330 hours, indicates that the Germans had come to the same conclusion:

'Enemy have so extended their penetration in I SS Panzerkorps sector by the capture of Grainville [and Tourmauville] at 1800 hrs that a breakthrough eastwards to capture Caen is to be expected'.

CHAPTER FIVE

Day 3 – Hill 112 and the German Counter-Attacks

On the night of 27 – 28 June 1944, *Feldmarshalls* von Rundstedt and Rommel, who had been summoned to the Eagle's Nest at Berchesgaden by Hitler, were discussing the situation in Normandy and the massed panzer counter-stroke. However, in the absence of both senior commanders, Headquarters C in C West's war diary recorded that:

'*Army Group B has instructed Seventh* Armee *to prevent this* [the British breakout] *and restore the situation by attacking with all available parts of II SS* Panzerkorps, *and 8* Werferbrigade.'

Consequently, General Dollman's Seventh *Armee* Headquarters issued orders to SS-*Obergruppenführer* Hauser, directing II SS *Panzerkorps* to the Odon Front. This was contrary to Hitler's intention, which was to use this *Korps* in the counter-stroke towards Bayeux. Under pressure, Dollman added the instruction that Hauser was 'to attack immediately in order to clear the breach south of Cheux'. Hauser reported that he was unable to attack before 29 June and that he would prefer to fight a holding action. At this point, unable to cope with the situation, Dollman committed suicide. This precipitated confusion and paralysis in the German command. Orders were not reviewed, as newly appointed commanders struggled to get to grips with inherited plans.

By mid afternoon, orders from Hitler were being circulated that SS-*Obergruppenführer* Hauser, was to assume command of Seventh *Armee* and, pending the return of von Rundstedt and Rommel, he was also to 'command the invasion front.' The resulting chain of moves saw SS-*Gruppenführer* Bittrich taking command of II SS *Panzerkorps*, while SS-*Standartenführer* Thomas Muller, left 20 Pz Gr Regt and took over 9th *Frundsberg* SS Panzer Division. At possibly the most crucial moment since D-Day, command arrangements in Germany's remaining full strength elite formation, were in turmoil. This had a significant impact on the battle that II SS *Panzerkorps* was to fight over the following days. As a final change, General Geyr von Schweppenburg's HQ *Panzergruppe* West was inserted between Hauser

SS-Obergruppenführer Paul Hauser.

SS-Obersturmbannführer Otto Weidinger commanded the battlegroup Kampfgruppe Weidinger.

at Seventh *Armee* and the field formations, taking command of the two SS *Panzerkorps*, XLVII Pz *Korps* and LXXXVI *Infantrie Korps*. General Geyr von Schweppenburg's area of responsibility roughly coincided with that of Second British Army.

At the tactical level, the *Hitlerjugend* was to be reinforced by further *kampfgruppen* rushing to face the threat posed by EPSOM. In addition to the Panthers of 2nd *Wien* Panzer Division which had already arrived, two battalions of the 1st SS *Leibstandarte* Panzer Division and *Kampfgruppe* Weidinger, from 2nd *Das Reich* SS Panzer Division, were due to arrive on 28 June. Kurt Meyer intended to use these reinforcements to attack from east and west and cut the 'Corridor'.

Rauray

At midnight on 27/28 June, a signal from XXX Corps to Second Army summarized:
'Intentions for 28 June. 49th Division is to

1 Tyneside Scottish, 49th Division.

capture Brettevillette using one Brigade supported by elements of 8
Armoured Brigade and by Corps Artillery. The Brigade group will then
reorganize in that area and patrol vigorously.'

At 0650 hours, the 'Polar Bears' artillery opened a ten minute barrage that preceded the attack by the Tyne Scots on Brettevillette. Opposition was brushed aside and, under cover of a creeping barrage, the battalion reached its initial objective of Bretteville in under an hour. Meanwhile, 11 DLI attacked south from Rauray to clear Point 110, which had been the source of so much trouble on 15th Scottish Division's western flank the day before. The DLI seized and held Point 110 but the Tyne Scots, now holding their subsequent objective of Brettevillette, were subjected to counter-attacks. They beat of the tired and, by now, disorganized *Hitlerjugend* but an attack by the fresh *Kampfgruppe* Weidinger (2nd *Das Reich* SS Panzer Division) newly arrived from St Lo, ejected the Tynesiders. However, other battalions of 49th Division had closed up behind them and with Point 110 in British hands the significant German tactical advantage of positions on the Rauray Spur had been removed. It had taken four day's of fighting.

Garvus

With a secure bridgehead over the Odon, VIII Corps confirmed that their intention for 28 June was:

> *'... to complete Phase 1* [secure the Gavrus Bridges] *and begin*
> *Phase 2 Operation EPSOM and secure the high ground north east of*
> *Bretteville sur Laize in order to cut roads leading south and south east*
> *from Caen'.*

Overnight, it will be recalled that 2 A&SH completed Phase 1 by dispatching platoon sized patrols to secure the bridges at Gavrus. On the morning of 28 June, with 159 Brigade now forming the bridgehead across the Orne, the remainder of the Argyles moved west to consolidate their hold on the two bridges. Corporal Campbell described the move up the Odon Valley as, 'very difficult; through thick mud and hedges. It took us two hours to cover a mile to the bridges.'

The Argyles forward companies had not been in the village of Gavrus for long before the Germans probed their positions. Anti-tank gun commander, Corporal Campbell recalled:

> *'We came under fire from armoured cars. Firing above us, we could*
> *feel the wind of their shot as they went over us and exploded above*
> *Battalion HQ in the village. We fired at the armoured car and he*
> *withdrew.*

> *'Half an hour later we were stood-to by a shout from the left*
> *"German Infantry." I could see ten Germans coming through the wood*
> *towards us. We were told pull back, which we did under MG fire. We*

took up a well-camouflaged position to cover the bridge itself and Battalion HQ.'

Hill 112

After a sleepless night in the Odon Bridgehead, shortly after dawn on 28 June 1944, 23 H spotted two enemy Mark IVs 'on the high ground above Eaquay'. They engaged them at a range of 1,200 yards, resulting in 'one tank being knocked-out and one being damaged'. These two tanks were a part of 5 *Kompanie*, 12 SS Pz Regt who had fought on the Rauray Spur during the previous three days. Now they were south of the Odon, leaguered, with their exhausted crews taking what rest they could. Otherwise, it was relatively quiet, as 4

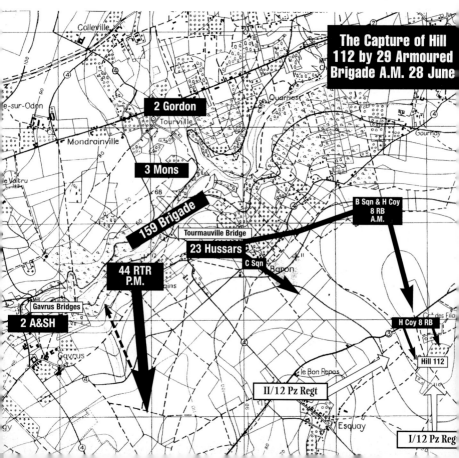

The Capture of Hill 112 by 29 Armoured Brigade A.M. 28 June

23 Hussars' Shermans and M3 half-tracks of 8 RB at the foot of Hill 112 in the Baron area.

KSLI's history describes:

> *Although no attack came in, a number of the enemy infiltrated between the company positions and made a nuisance of themselves. They first crept up and attacked the RAP [Regimental Aid Post] at a range of about thirty yards, wounding two stretcher-bearers. The reaction of the battalion was fierce, resulting in the expenditure of large*

A squadron of 23 Hussars' Shermans provide cover for the advance of the battlegroup towards Hill 112.

Having replenished their ammunition stocks, British Shermans deploy into their assault formation.

quantities of ammunition with little to show for it. These were early days and the battalion was still green. It was soon realized, however, that indiscriminate fire against stray Germans in close country was of little value, and later these men – they were called snipers although they were very ordinary German infantry with the most rudimentary ideas of musketry – were hunted by small parties of men with more success, about ten of them being killed or captured.'

Meanwhile, leaving 159 Infantry Brigade to hold the Bridgehead, 29 Armoured Brigade advanced south towards Hills 112 and 113 and the Orne. 23 H's Commanding Officer, taking advantage of the Germans' relative inactivity, dispatched B Squadron to the top of Hill 112. However, a *Luftwaffe* motorised flak battery, I/53, was deployed around the feature, with its 88mm guns in the ground role. In addition, 11th Armoured Division's war diary is littered with reports of tank v tank engagements, as 29 Brigade attempted to push south. It was already obvious that the Orne could only be reached after a serious fight. The Hussar's historian wrote that:

> *'C Squadron remained where they were to give B Squadron covering*

fire as they moved forward. Skirting the ruins of Baron, B Squadron approached the hill from the north as the lie of the ground gave most cover for an approach from that direction and most of the enemy fire seemed to be coming from the western slope of the hill. They went for some time over open, undulating country, which was good going for tanks, reminiscent of the Yorkshire Wolds. One tank was hit by a 50 millimetre shot, which broke its track, and Lieutenant. Cochrane's tank was hit and destroyed. The crew got out and came under heavy fire from both sides... The Squadron had meanwhile, by moving round a little further to the east, had established itself on the northern part of the hill. The enemy opposition in the area consisted of dug-in tanks and infantry in positions in a small wood. Their tanks had alternative sites to move to under cover and were almost impossible to get at. An attempt was made to knock them out with some self-propelled anti-tank guns which were under our command and were sent forward with B Squadron. It was unsuccessful. Medium artillery was tried without effect. Finally, rocket firing Typhoons were called up but the Tigers [more probably Mark IVs and Panthers of 12 SS Pz Regt] were well camouflaged and the pilots were unable to locate them. The Gunners put down red smoke to indicate the target. One round fell amongst our own tanks and the

A 75mm anti-tank gun, crewed by SS gunners, in action against advancing enemy armour.

An abandoned German 88mm gun in the Hill 112 area.

hillside was immediately covered in yellow smoke, tins of which were issued to each tank so that it could signal to our aircraft and assure them that it was friendly. It often worked. On this occasion, the CO dropped the smoke in the turret of his tank to the great amusement of those who were near enough to see what happened and the discomfiture of his crew who found it rather overpowering.'

C Squadron eventually joined B Squadron on the northern slope of Hill 112, along with Regimental HQ 23 H and H Company 8 RB. At 1235 hours, 29 Armoured Brigade were reporting that they were 'almost entirely on Pt 112 feature except for western slope'. However, despite much manoeuvring and firing, the out-ranged Hussars could not overcome the interlocking arcs of the 88mm anti-tank guns and losses of Shermans mounted. Smoke from burning tanks, including the Commanding Officer's tank, started to billow across the battlefield. H Company was sent forward to take the orchard on the top of the hill, which it did, despite taking casualties. Rifleman Roland Jefferson recalls,

A Nebelwerfer being loaded with its 150mm projectiles.

'Hill 112 will always be remembered as our initiation into the real hatefulness of war. We found ourselves in a cornfield protecting the [western] flanks overlooking the valley leading to Esquay.'

It would appear that the hilltop was held by the equivalent of a company of *Hitlerjugend* panzer grenadiers, who along with the anti-tank gunners fell back as the British infantry advanced on them.

The news of the British capture of Hill 112 was

passed to 8 *Werferbrigade* by field telephone. *Feldwebel* Doorn, who answered the telephone, ran to get 6 Battery's commander, who received the following message:

'Sir, the British are on top of the hill. A Sherman tank has stopped just five metres from one of our observation posts. For God's sake don't ring – they'll hear it. We'll try and get back somehow. I don't know what has happened to Leutnant *Wernike and* Leutnant *Nitschmann. I think they must have been overrun.'*

'In order to confirm what was happening, Feldwebel *Doorn was dispatched with a patrol up the open southern slopes of the hill but he was driven off loosing two men. His report to* Hauptmann *Gengl confirmed: 'It's not just a couple of tanks up there! Tommy's got anti-tank guns and part of a machine gun unit.'*

SS-*Obersturmbannführer* Max Wünsche planned a quick counter-attack to be delivered by his panzers. The Panthers of I/Battalion attacked from the south, while Mark IVs of II/Battalion advanced up the hill from the south west. SS-*Oberscharführer* Willy Kretzchmar, aged twenty, commanded one of the panzers climbing the slope from Esquay.

**SS-Obersturmbannführer
Max Wünsche**

'After a short assembly, we started the attack in a broad wedge formation on that wooded area. We worked our way forward, each panzer giving the other covering fire. Without obvious targets, we fired armour piercing and HE shells into the wood. The attack moved forward briskly. When we had approached to within 300 to 400 m, we spotted retreating English soldiers between the trees. We fired the turret and hull machine guns into the wood.

*'I was now the point panzer. Our advance was roughly north west ... We cautiously made our way forward through the small wood. When we came to the end of the cover provided by the little wood, I had an observation halt. With my binoculars, I searched the country stretching away to our left, looking for tanks and anti-tank guns. Nothing suspicious! "Panzer advance!" I shouted. We had advanced ten or fifteen metres when there was a sudden crash. The sparks flew. We had been hit from the right. "Reverse" I shouted. SS-*Sturmmann *Schneider reacted with lightning speed. Back we shot at full speed. Back into cover of the wood. Not one second too soon! The Englander almost*

> got us! A hairs-breadth in front of our panzer, armour-piercing solid
> shot was tearing ugly black furrows in the green grass.'

The *Hitlerjugend's* counter-attack was beaten off but not before they knocked out further Shermans, some of whom had just arrived as battle-casualty replacements from the Armoured Delivery Squadron. Despite their failure to retake Hill 112, the ring of panzers and the remaining Luftwaffe 88mm guns, to the south of the feature, 'roped-off the British advance'. In these circumstances, the 23 H battlegroup could not reach the Orne without further support. At 1445 hours, 44 RTR came under command of 29 Armoured Brigade and attempted to advance south to Hill 113 but mutually supporting anti-tank fire prevented a significant advance. However, I SS *Panzerkorps*, focusing on their vital ground, was not content with containing the British; they wanted Hill 112, 'the cornerstone of our defences in Normandy', back in their possession. The young soldiers of 12 SS Pz Regt were to counter-attack again. SS-*Obersturmführer* Kandler of 5 *Kompanie* was with them:

> 'My gunner, Willi Schnittfinke, reported a defect in the electric
> firing mechanism. We had to halt, and after a quick repair, we were some
> distance behind the three panzers manoeuvring in front of us. SS
> Sturmbannführer *Mueller was also hanging back behind Porsch and*
> Kunze. Kunze, in the leading panzer, referring no doubt to those
> hanging back, shouted over the wireless: "It's all the bloody same to me!
> Advance!" Two hundred yards from the little wood Kunze's panzer was
> knocked out. Only the gunner and driver baled out. Groeter, the driver,
> was visibly shaken. He said the shell had gone clean between his legs.'

Another counter-attack had failed.

After almost twelve hours in action on Hill 112, the Hussars needed an 'ammunition replen' but in broad daylight, it was impossible to bring the trucks forward. Therefore, at about 1500 hours they were relieved by A Squadron 3 RTR. Major Bill Close described this as 'A rather daunting proposition, as we moved through some of the burnt out tanks of the Hussars'. They had lost thirty-three troopers killed in action, thirty-three wounded and six missing. Taking a route through Baron, 3 RTR came under 'intense tank fire' that cost them their first tank loss of the campaign. Once on the Hill Lieutenant Langdon commented:

> 'We remained in these rather negative positions for the remainder of
> the day. We were able to knock out several anti-tank guns but could
> make no impression on the dug-in Tiger tanks.'

Sergeant Caswell was with B Squadron 3 RTR on the eastern flank of Hill 112, and summed up why the Germans regarded Hill 112 as vital ground:

> 'My tank had a wonderful position from which we could see
> Carpiquet airfield, the whole of Caen and to the east the river Orne and

The shell scared Hill 112. Photographed during late June 1944.

the Borgubeus ridge six miles to the east.'

G Company 8 RB joined 3 RTR on Hill 112. Rifleman Norman Habertin recalls that shortly after their arrival on the hilltop:

'The storm broke. The enemy had been watching us settle down and before a single trench had been dug, down came those dreaded "moaning minnies". There was nothing to do but lie down and bite the earth. A *half-track a few yards away went up in flames and when the mortaring finally stopped, the complete battalion was in a state of utter chaos. All the company vehicles were mixed up, no one knew where their section or platoon was, wounded men were yelling for help and nobody in authority could get any orders carried out.'*

8 RB were not the only occupants of Hill 112 and it was not long before the British infantry discovered that some enemy bunkers were still occupied.

'Suddenly a scraggy-looking beggar in field grey appeared from a hedge hatless and with his hands in the air. He was rushed off at the point of a bayonet. He kept looking back, frightened or perhaps worried about what was happening to his companions. A moment later, two more, one an officer, were captured.'

These *Wehrmacht* officers, possibly *Leutnant* Wernike and *Leutnant* Nitschmann were 6 *Werferbatterie's* forward observation officers, who had been overrun. Sheltering in their well-prepared dugouts, they had been able to call down fire on their own positions. However, failing to force the British off the hillside, they surrendered.

Despite losses of almost forty Shermans, the British position on the northern edge of Hill 112 seemed secure but 29 Armoured Brigade's positions were surrounded on three sides. In addition, they were at the end of a very exposed corridor, which was in places, little more than a mile wide. Lieutenant General O'Connor, commander VIII Corps, and Montgomery himself, must have been acutely aware of this as they digested the flash signal from ULTRA: Rommel had authorized the release of the forty thousand men of II SS *Panzerkorps*. This powerful formation was to attack the British salient from the west and destroy VIII Corps. 11th Armoured Division's positions in the Odon bridgehead and on Hill 112 were dangerously exposed.

At 1945 hours, with senior British commanders beginning to doubt the wisdom of holding their foothold on Hill 112, a watchkeeper recorded in 11th Armoured Division's war diary that '29 Armoured Brigade report all quiet but 3 RTR heavily engaged if they move forward'. However, at 2150 hours, the Germans attacked again and it was recorded that 'Royal Artillery report engaging tanks forming up for attack in Esquay'. The artillery failed to break up the attack and the enemy surrounding the Hill 112 closed in.

'2200 hours. 29 Armoured Brigade report 3 Tigers have appeared on the Hill 112 feature. There is also sniper and machine gun fire coming from Esquay. We [Brigade Headquarters] are being engaged. The situation concerning 3 RTR is slightly confused.'

The accompanying panzer grenadiers advanced up onto Hill 112, forcing G Company, 8 RB to be withdrawn, leaving only a foothold on the northern edge of the plateau but the counter-attack was halted. Lieutenant Langdon of 12 Troop, 3 RTR, wrote that:

> 'We remained in position on the hill for 36 hours. That first night was most unpleasant. We more or less stood to in our tanks as we were practically surrounded.'

Hill 112 was already littered with the wrecks of knocked-out armoured vehicles and the bodies of British and German soldiers. For both sides Hill 112 was to become the most notorious spot on the Normandy front. Hill 112 did not to finally fall to the British until 23 August.

The *Leibstandarte's* Counter-Attack

While 11th Armoured Division and the *Hitlerjugend* spent the day locked in battle on Hill 112, there were serious developments on the flanks of the Corridor. During the night of 27 – 28 June, welcome reinforcements came under command of the *Hitlerjugend*. SS-*Standartenführer* Kurt Meyer was not going to allow a repeat of the previous day's debacle when the Panther's of 2nd *Wien* Panzer Division attacked Cheux without infantry support. He planned properly coordinated and supported attacks from east and west along the Caen–Villers-Bocage road, designed to cut the Scottish Corridor and isolate 11th Armoured Division in the Odon Bridgehead, where II SS *Panzerkorps* would destroy them.

Approaching from the east, the two leading battalions of SS-*Obersturmbannführer* Albert Frey's 1 SS Pz Gr Regt, were particularly welcome as the *Hitlerjugend* was critically short of infantry. However, starved of fuel and harried by Allied fighter bombers, it would take a week

A Leibstandarte officer during the fighting in Normandy.

before the remainder of the *Leibstandarte* was complete on the Caen front. Joining *Kampfgruppe* Frey were the *Wehrmacht* Mark IVs of 4 *Kompanie* and five Panthers of 7 *Kompanie* 22 Pz Regt and three Tigers from 101 SS *Schwerepanzer* Battalion. This *kampfgruppe* was to attack from Verson westward towards Colleville.

Taking part in the attack on the western side of the Scottish Corridor was another SS *kampfgruppe,* under the command of SS-*Standartenführer* Weidinger. This *kampfgruppe* was made up from 2nd *Das Reich* SS *Panzer* Division's leading units, which were arriving from south western France. Moving east under cover of night, they had assembled in Noyers in order to attack the Corridor from the west.

Positioned astride the Caen–Villers-Bocage Road were the fresh troops of Brigadier Carver's 4 Armoured Brigade (less 44 RTR). Also in the area to face the German counter-attacks, were a mixture of units, from 11th Armoured and 15th Scottish Divisions, many of whom were fighting under command of an unfamiliar headquarters.

SS-*Obersturmbannführer* Frey was not, however, happy with the arrangements for what he considered to be a precipitate attack on the eastern side of the Corridor. He later wrote:

> 'I received the attack order from SS-Standartenführer *Kurt Meyer*. I immediately made him aware that I could not execute the order without the support of heavy weapons. I therefore requested a delay until the Leibstandarte's *artillery could arrive. He answered my objection by saying that the artillery of 12th SS Pz Division would support my attack.'*

The *Leibstandarte's* attack began at 0600 hours, with the panzer grenadiers leading the tanks through the hedges and small fields of the Bocage country towards Mouen and Tourville. The railway and the road were used as the axis of advance. SS-*Obersturmbannführer* Frey complained:

> 'I started the attack at the designated time but it was with a heavy heart that I gave the order. As I had feared, there was no artillery observation officer with me and 12th SS Artillery did not take any action of its own accord. The enemy offered immediate and heavy resistance. A remarkable feature of the resistance was the machine gun fire. It was very heavy and fell with intensity along the entire attack sector. It appeared that they were firing it from tanks.'

SS-Obersturmbannführer Albert Frey commanded the counter-attack by the Leibstandarte.

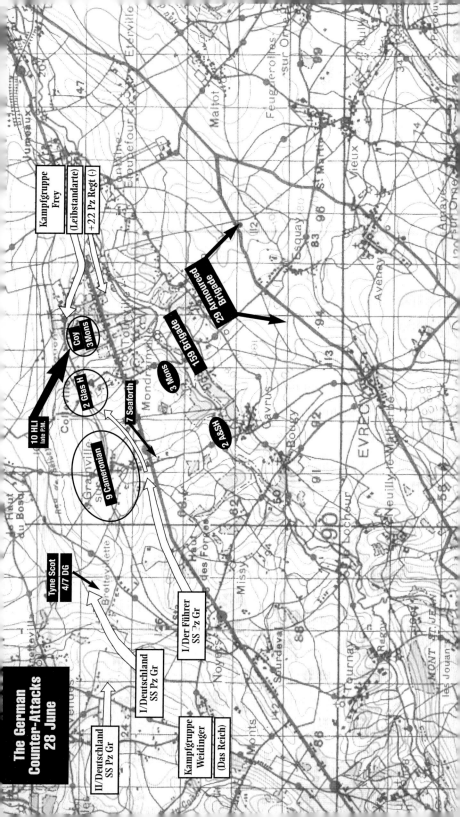

The German
Counter-Attacks
28 June

Kampfgruppe
Frey

(Leibstandarte)
+22 Pz Regt (-)

10 HLI
late P.M.

Coy
3 Mons

2 Glas H

7 Seaforth

9 Cameronian

3 Mons

159 Brigade

29 Armoured
Brigade

2 A&SH

Tyne Scot
4/7 DG

1/Der Führer
SS Pz Gr

1/Deutschland
SS Pz Gr

II/Deutschland
SS Pz Gr

Kampfgruppe
Weidinger

(Das Reich)

For a second time German battle procedure had fallen bellow expectation. However, the advance, despite initial surprise, made slow progress forward against the isolated C Company 3 Monmouths and tanks of 3 County of London Yeomanry (3 CLY). Lieutenant Kendall was a Mons platoon commander. He explained that:

> 'We then started to consolidate according to orders and I gave a few directions before sitting down near a ruined house for some tea and consulting my map. A moment or so later some of our chaps at the end of the village ran up to say Jerries were coming. We barely had time to get to our feet before they were upon us, tanks and half-tracks and other stuff, all firing like mad. There was a wild scramble for cover with stuff flying everywhere and the buildings were being torn to pieces by shellbursts. In a matter of seconds, the Jerries were in amongst us and it was hell, pandemonium and a terrific, deafening noise. I tried to get behind a wall but was hit.'

Lieutenant Kendal played dead and had to endure the British bombardment, before he was found by counter-attacking Jocks. Three days later he was back in England, having had his leg amputated. Private Evans also fought with C Company:

> 'We were not properly dug-in. Many were killed or wounded in the heavy bombardment. A light recce tank arrived – one of ours [3 CLY]. "Get back, they've got heavy tanks!" we shouted. But it stayed and was soon hit and in flames.'

Commanding a Mark IV in the attack was Werner Kortenhaus of 4 *Kompanie* 22 Pz Regt, who recalled that:

> 'We advanced in the morning, moving along the railway line with the grenadiers. The Panther tanks were further left. My Kompanie had five operational panzers in action. Almost immediately, we ran into

Shermans of 4th Armoured Brigade moving forward on the cleared route around Cheux. Note the mine tape.

A MkIV belonging to II/22 Pz Regt knocked out while supporting the Leibstandarte. This obsolescent tank would probably have been issued as a replacement from a training unit; it has the short 75mm gun.

fierce opposition. The SS grenadiers came and asked us to help them. They said that they had surrounded a company of British infantry in Mouen.'

C Company 3 Mons fought on but were pushed back by superior numbers and a lack of support until they were overwhelmed. Major Richards and fourteen soldiers escaped, twenty-three were killed and the remainder or taken prisoner by the *Leibstandarte*. Amongst the prisoners was Private Evans who wrote that:

'We looked after our wounded as best we could. We carried one on a door used as a stretcher. Later the SS general saw some of his soldiers taking our cigarettes. He was very angry. He pointed to our [11th Armoured Division] shoulder flashes, said something and made them give the cigarettes back. His name was Kurt something or other [Meyer?]. He was a gentleman.'

With C Company 3 Mons overwhelmed in Mouen, the *Leibstandarte's* next objective was Colleville. 2 Glas H. were holding the village and the vital route south to the Tourmauville Bridge. The *Leibstandarte* attacked late in the morning from Mouen but despite securing footholds in Colleville, the SS were driven back by local counter-attacks during the afternoon. Despite failing to cut the Corridor, the *Leibstandarte* had dangerously narrowed the British salient. 'To clear up this situation 10 HLI put in an attack on Mouen at 1945 hours supported by a squadron of tanks.'

10 HLI advanced 'in open formation', with A Company left and D right, followed respectively by C and B Companies. The Shermans of the County of London Yeomanry moved on either side of the HLI. Private Arkwright, who was with the assault infantry, recalled:

'They told us we could now get the SS buggers and take care of them. So we perked up a bit and got ready, and soon after that two sergeants led us off carrying Stens and soon we went into the fields. There was some corn and a few bushes and then we heard shouts and bangs and we dashed forward firing like mad and yelling our heads off.'

Advancing through the waist high corn from the area north of Cheux towards the railway line, the HLI came under heavy machine gun fire and the accompanying tanks were engaged by anti-tank guns. The Battalion's war diary entry for 2015 hours recorded:

'A-Tk gunfire aimed at tanks on left. One Sherman knocked-out. Heavy MG fire from houses and railway sweeping top of corn. A and B Coys & Bn HQ pinned down by MG fire & unable to advance. Five Panthers destroyed. three Shermans knocked-out.

'On right: D & B advanced down right of railway towards wood. Before reaching wood came under heavy MG fire from Panther tank, dug-in in the orchard. OC Coy wounded, two subalterns killed. Unable to advance owing to the MG fire sweeping open ground. Withdrew to sunken lane.'

With the advance on the right flank was Private Arkwright, who continued his account:

'It was fantastic but terrible, as we saw all these bodies of our own chaps and Jerries with brown camouflage jackets, some dead, some wounded, some firing or trying to get away. We showed no mercy at all; we fired in all directions and just wiped out the lot. We were so worked up into a rage.

'When we got through their first position we soon came under fire from elsewhere, so we dug ourselves in. I felt completely worn out and all in a sweat, and I kept seeing all those poor Jocks lying dead and I felt sick and cried.'

Still in action at Mouen with *Kampfgruppe* Frey was Werner Kortenhaus of 4 *Kompanie* 22 Pz Regt, who recalled that:

'We received a direct hit. The battle had suddenly flared up again. We couldn't traverse the gun. The turret was jammed. As we pulled back, we were hit again, this time in the rear. Fortunately, the shot bounced off. An hour later, with the turret freed we were back in the thick of the action. One of our panzers was in flames. Another slowly

backed out of the battle with the commander, Eichler, lying dead in the turret. He had been decapitated by a shell as he was looking over the top. A third was hit.'

After several further determined attempts to take Mouen from the west, 10 HLI was ordered to pull back at dusk. According to 227 Brigade's war diary, the Battalion 'dug-in for the night in a position a few hundred yards from their start line'. Both sides had lost heavily in the battle on the eastern flank on 28 June but above all, SS-*Obersturmbannführer* Frey's attack had failed to cut the Corridor and the *Leibstandarte* were now struggling to hold their limited gains. At this point, 43rd Wessex Division was ordered to take responsibility for the eastern flank and improve the situation before the full weight of II SS *Panzerkorp's* expected counter-attack fell on the Corridor.

Das Reich's Counter-Attack

During the course of 28 June, *Kampfgruppe* Weidinger, with Mondrainville as its objective, mounted the second part of the counter-attack north of the Odon. With a Panther company in support, the panzer grenadiers of 1st Battalion *Deutschland*, on the left, attacked Brettevillet and the Rauray Spur, while 1st Battalion *Der Führer,* on the right, ran into British positions in Grainville.

At Brettevillet the Tyneside Scottish, supported by Shermans of B Squadron 4th/7th Dragoon Guards, who had been advancing south towards the hamlet, clashed with I/*Deutschland* in an encounter battle. Captain Whitehead wrote:

> *'Ground was being made and by 1430 hours, all companies were on their objectives but were engaged in stiff fighting in Brettevillette where they were being counter-attacked in considerable strength by the 2nd SS Panzer Division infantry and tanks. Very confused fighting continued in the village. It was evident that it would not be possible to hold it and the CO ordered the companies back – D Company being only 300 yards from the built-up area.'*

The Tyneside Scottish suffered one hundred and twenty-six casualties; however, I/*Deutschland* also suffered particularly heavy casualties during the battle for Brettevillet. As the British bombardment persisted, wounded SS were still being carried to the rear well into the evening. There was to be no further advance on *Kampfgruppe* Weidenger's left flank on evening of 28 June.

On the *Kampfgruppe's* right flank, advancing along the main road to Caen, I/*Das Führer* came under fire from Grainville, to the north of the road, which, unknown to Weidinger, was occupied by 9 Cameronians.

Flammenpanzer III. These older models were given a new lease of life by the conversion to flame projectors.

Sometime later, to the south of the road, they encountered 7 Seaforth in a meeting engagement at le Valtru. Supporting 46 (Highland) Brigade's infantry battalions were A and B Squadrons of 9 RTR. The country in which the battle took place was typical bocage, with small fields surrounded by hedged earth banks and sunken lanes.

In this thick country, battle was a matter of infiltration and all round defence rather than bold speedy attacks. For the infantry, it was *Nebelwerfers* and rifle fire, resulting in heavy casualties. For the RTR's Churchills, it was a difficult and deadly business. Lieutenant Peter Beal wrote:

> *'Shortly after 8 and 10 Troops had reached Grainville, Teddy Mott's 9 Troop was sent round to the south of the village to clear its southern flank. But in a hedgerow a German tank waited unseen until Teddy was 100 yards or so away and then opened fire. Teddy's driver and gunner were both killed and the other two wounded. Teddy's legs were smashed below the knee. He managed to get out of the tank but left one leg on the track guard and had the other amputated after he crawled back through the fields and had been taken by ambulance jeep to the medical services.'*

Lieutenant Mott's Troop Sergeant, George Rathke, recalled seeing his Troop Commander's tank 'Inspire' being hit:

> *'... there was a big flash and Inspire was hit, flames belching out of the turret. Then I heard a shell, presumably aimed at my tank, whistle overhead. I had by then told my wireless-op to send out smoke from the 2-inch mortar; I also directed my gunner on the spot where I thought the shots were coming from, and we fired two AP rounds and began to*

reverse having concealed ourselves in smoke.

'Having reversed about 100 yards, I halted and looked for survivors. I spotted Jimmy Deem running towards some other tanks of the squadron among the orchards. Suddenly several German machine guns opened on him and he fell to the ground. We engaged the machine guns with Bessa and fired a couple of HE shells into the hedgerows concealing the German machine guns. All this happened in a matter of minutes – which seemed like hours.'

The infantry held their positions in the villages and in the surrounding orchards and hedgerows but, in a running short range duel, I/*Der Führer* and some Panthers penetrated between Grainville and le Valtru towards Collevile and Mondrainville. Sergeant Green was with 10 HLI near Colleville:

'To all intents and purposes, we were out of the battle. Heavy fire from the direction of le Valtru caused havoc to the trucks of A1 Echelon, which carried the most urgently needed supplies, and when a heavy German attack developed against le Valtru itself we could see two German flame-throwing tanks in action and machine gun fire was incessant. Walking wounded came streaming back along the embankment, and our battalion stood by to seal off penetration, but gradually the position was restored and the fire slackened. A nasty situation had been developing but despite being over-run by enemy tanks, the infantry held firm and the Germans were driven out.'

Das Reich's part of the attack had also failed. The ground was unfavourable and the volume of British artillery fire was, as ever, a significant factor but *Kampfgruppe* Weidinger had also lacked sufficient combat power to stand a realistic chance of breaking through to the *Leibstandarte*.

Hill 112

With the Corridor north of the Odon under pressure and II SS *Panzerkorps* approaching the Normandy front, Lieutenant General O'Connor permitted the withdrawal of 29 Armoured Brigade from the crest of Hill 112. Major Noel Bell of 8 RB describes the operation:

'There was much confusion. Nobody seemed to be sure what was

happening or what the form was. Brian approached, supported under the arms by two of his section leaders. The parts of his face not covered with blood showed through deathly pale. We gave him a shot of brandy from a flask; he coughed. The trucks and carriers made their way back through the orchard. We saw a half-track burning, one of H Company's. Ammunition was exploding and the burning tyres made vivid circles of flames. We made lagger, and attempted to find order out of chaos. A feeling of depression swept through us. There were only two officers left. The morning just a few hours behind us, seemed another age.'

In summary, 28 June had dawned with 11th Armoured Division having a real chance of reaching the Orne and the open country beyond but ended with the Division being contained in a bridgehead that included Hill 112's northern slope. However, the timely and, as the Germans say, piecemeal arrival of reinforcing SS *kampfgruppen*, had not only threatened the Corridor but had allowed the *Hitlerjugend* to redeploy south of the Odon to contain 11th Armoured Division on Hill 112. The delay that the Germans had inflicted on the 49th Division and 15th Scottish bought time for the arrival of forces for their planned counter-stroke.

Armoured vehicles of 29 Armoured Brigade withdrawing from Hill 112 via Baron.

CHAPTER SIX

Day 4 – II SS *Panzerkorps'* Counter-Attack

The Second Army war diary records a message from General O'Connor at HQ VIII Corps, timed shortly after midnight:

> *'Intention for 29 Jun 44. First. To enlarge bridgehead over the ODON. Second, 15 Div to clear general area COLLEVILLE-TOURVILLE-TOURMAUVILLE-GARVUS-BOUCY WOODS (901628). Third. 43 Div to clear area including BAS DE MOUEN-GOURNAY. Fourth. 11 Armd Div will as soon as 15 and 43 Divs' tasks have been accomplished continue advance to R ORNE in accordance with original plan.*

At dawn on 29 June, the 'tidying-up' of the centre and flanks of the Corridor was already under way by the Wessex Division on the eastern flank and by the Scots to the west

Mouen

The village of Mouen needed to be cleared, as the Corridor was only 3,000 yards wide and if VIII Corps was to survive the coming counter-attack, it would need additional depth to absorb the German attacks. Mouen, lying between the railway line and the Caen– Villers-Bocage Road, was a small hamlet in close country, bisected by three deep, hedged lanes.

A lane in Mouen. Poor tank country.

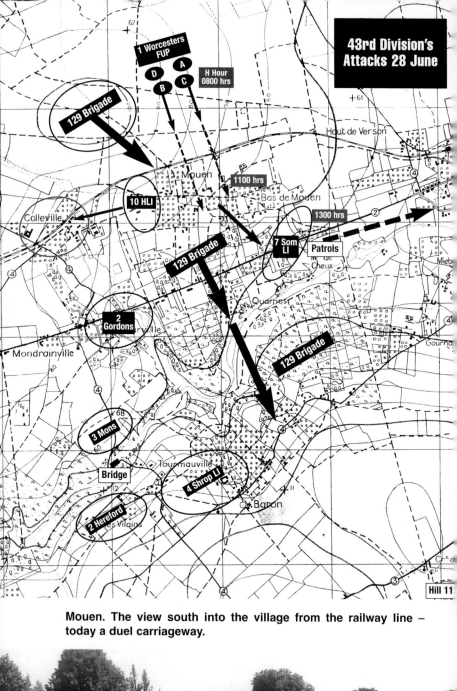

43rd Division's Attacks 28 June

1 Worcesters FUP

D   A
B   C

H Hour 0800 hrs

129 Brigade

Hout de Verson

Mouen

1100 hrs

Bas de Mouen

10 HLI

1300 hrs

Colleville

129 Brigade

7 Som LI

Patrols

Mieb

M. de Cheux

Quarries

2 Gordons

ville

Gourn

Mondrainville

129 Brigade

3 Mons

Bridge

Tourmauville

4 Shrop LI

Baron

2 Hereford

les Vilains

Hill 11

Mouen. The view south into the village from the railway line – today a duel carriageway.

Transport belonging to 43rd Wessex Division, south of Cheux, moving up to the battle area.

It will be recalled that the village had been occupied with out a fight by 3 Mons, as the result of a map reading error on the night of the 27/28 June. However, the following day it had been lost to the counter-attacking *Leibstandarte* and 10 HLI had been unable to retake it. At 2000 hours the previous evening, the Wessex Division's 214 Brigade had been ordered forward to take the village but only two hours of daylight remained. Brigadier Essame recalled:

'In hope of being able to exploit the [limited] *success of the HLI by passing through them and carrying Mouen by a night assault, I moved 1 Worcester to an assembly area in the fields south of Cheux. Accompanied by the CO, Lt Col Harrison, and Major Alexander, his battery commander, I then went forward to reconnoitre, turned off the axis just north of Colleville and followed in the wake of 10 HLI. Amongst the high hedges and meadows we found the battalion grimly fighting its way forward inch by inch and at a heavy cost ...*

'Back amongst the tightly packed traffic on the axis, I decided that a night advance through the HLI with the enemy still holding out in the

narrow fields and orchards could only end in confusion and that an assault at first light from the north over the open fields would be more effective.

'My Brigade O Group assembled at 3.30 a.m. by the light of a pressure lamp in a 160-lb tent near le Gaule. 1 Worcester were to seize Mouen by an attack from the open cornfields on the extreme east flank of the corridor and to exploit as far as the main road to Caen. No tanks were available but... 179 Field Regiment, in addition to the whole Divisional artillery who had secured the support of two medium regiments.'

Into the morning mist. British infantry advance towards the German positions.

1 Worcester had been ordered to capture Mouen by 0900 hours. Time was short, so it was impossible for Lieutenant Colonel Harrison and Major Alexander to recce the ground, make a plan and be ready by the given H-hour of 0800. The plan, made from the map, required careful co-ordination with the artillery. According to the battalion history, the fire plan called:

'... for a barrage of HE with smoke mixed, opening on the line of the railway short of the village of Mouen, dwelling there for thirty minutes (which was the estimated time for the advance across the open country), then moving forward at 100 yards in four minutes to the main Caen road. ... The mortars of the Battalion were to take on opportunity targets and those of 7th Somerset Light Infantry to fire phosphorous smoke into the barrage both for blinding and lethal effect. 4.2 inch mortars were to fire smoke and HE on Bas-de-Mouen which appeared the obvious line of counter-attack and the medium machine guns were to fire on Carpiquet Aerodrome not only to

146

The pylon line used by 1 Worcesters as its axis during the attack on Mouen.

neutralize but also a deception.'

For simplicity Lieutenant Colonel Harrison planned to use obvious features; the advance was to be astride a line of pylons leading towards the church in Mouen which was the second landmark. B Company was on the right and C Company on the left. A Company was in support, moving on the left in order to cover the open flank and was, subsequently, to seize Bas-de-Mouen. D Company was the Battalion's reserve. The well rehearsed battle procedure 'went like clockwork' and the attack began on time.

> *'The battalion moved forward through the cornfield in copybook style. Not a man seemed out of place and never had the Battalion gone into attack so well in any training.'*

However, the Worcesters suffered some shrapnel casualties from enemy airburst shells but officers and NCOs kept the men moving forward 'in a very open formation', which minimized casualties. Brigadier Essame also wrote that the Germans:

> *'Deceived by the smoke as to the direction of the attack, the enemy put down his defensive fire not on the Worcesters but on the right flank, the direction from which it had been intended to assault the previous night.'*

Regimental Sergeant Major Hurd was 'well to the fore brandishing a shovel and calling on the troops to close with the enemy, advanced behind the barrage'. A reason for the Worcesters' success in crossing the open ground was that they followed the barrage closely, as it moved into the German positions and being on top of the enemy when he emerged from his cover.

The Worcesters' battle with the panzer grenadiers and tanks of Hitler's *Leibstandarte* began at the edge of the village. According to Major Watson:

> *'Some opposition from automatic fire was met with on coming to the railway line, but our artillery had opened very accurately on that line and neutralized most opposition there. However, directly we got over the line they found themselves in real close country, consisting of small*

fields with high hedges and sunken lanes. In these hedges, lanes and in the tops of trees, there was still a large number of Germans very much alive. Progress forward was slow, as each little orchard had to be dealt with separately before going on to the next if control was to be retained. In addition, there were some enemy tanks, which had been dug-in in the narrow lanes and were being used as pillboxes.'

Young Worcester soldiers armed with PIATs crept forward, uncertain how the ungainly spring propelled weapon would work against a real tank. Covered by the fire of the remainder of their platoon, they crawled into positions from where they could engage the SS panzers, including at least one Tiger, in their vulnerable flanks. They were greatly heartened to see the 'steel monsters burst into flames'. The PIAT proved to be equally effective in blasting the determined SS defenders out of hedgerow positions and from buildings. However, progress through the village was much slower than the rate of advance of 100 yards in four minutes cited in the artillery fire plan. At 1100, hours the Battalion reached their limit of exploitation short of the Caen–Villers Road.

Mouen was not a pretty sight, being littered with knocked-out armour, dead Monmouths and bodies of the HLI, all the product of the previous day's fighting. However, the Worcesters were extremely thorough in their clearing of the village. This resulted in the Battalion suffering relatively few

British soldiers inspect one of 101 SS Schwere Panzer Battalion's Tigers knocked out in the Mouen area.

casualties both during the attack and during the reorganization. In praising the attack, Montgomery described the Worcester's attack as 'The finest single action of the war'. 7 Som LI, moving through the village behind the Worcesters, was able to continue the attack towards the main road promptly, in good order and without significant casualties.

With the Worcester's success, 129 Brigade advanced between Mouen and Colleville and down into the Odon Valley. Brigadier Essame recorded that:

'Relieved of responsibility for St Mauvieu by 2 Guards Brigade, [129 Brigade] now advanced in the late morning with a squadron of Greys under command, with the task of clearing the woods and orchards astride the River Odon between Tourville and Baron on the Corps' left flank. Deployed on a two battalion front, 5 Wiltshire on the right and 4 Somerset Light Infantry on the left, we advanced over the railway and past Colleville under heavy mortar fire until the ribbon of houses along the main road to Caen was reached. Here the battalions paused to reorganize and then thrust forward into the thick woods ahead. We reached the Odon and found it to be little more than a stream, but sufficient to hold up our carriers and anti-tank guns. On the right, the pioneers of 5 Wiltshire built a crossing of brushwood and earth. On the left 4 SLI found that the stream ran through a deep gorge and except for a narrow strip of grass either side was steep-sided, rocky and heavily wooded. This was to earn the name of 'Death Valley' in the days ahead.'

To the west of the Wessex, 44 (Lowland) Brigade was also ordered to improve the 15th's tenuously held positions on the northern slopes of the Odon. In order to widen the Corridor, by 1040 hours 8 Royal Scots secured, with little opposition, positions on the railway to the west of Grainville. In the next phase of the plan 6 Royal Scots Fusiliers began an advanced towards the Caen– Villers-Bocage Road and onwards to link up with the isolated Argyles at Gavrus. Meanwhile, in the early afternoon, 8 RS, who were digging-in, came under heavy mortar fire and attack by SS troopers who infiltrated through the wooded country. 6 RSF, still short of Gavrus, were redirected back to deal with this new threat. Thus, 44 Brigade was to clear the enemy from the area between Grainville and Gavrus and therefore, could not form a coherent defensive flank. This left the Argyles still isolated at Gavrus.

44 RTR's Advance on Hill 113

While the Wessex and Scottish Divisions were 'tidying up the Odon Valley', 11th Armoured Division started 29 June with the aim of reaching the Orne and an H-Hour of 0700 hours. From the western portion of the bridgehead, 44 RTR, under command of 29 Armoured Brigade, was again to advance south towards Hill 113 and Esquay. Accompanied by B Company 2 King's Royal Rifle Corps, C Squadron was directed on Hill 113. B Squadron moved on Evrecy, while A Squadron shot up Esquay.

Preparing to attack over the same ground, were the leading elements of the newly arrived II SS *Panzerkorps*. SS-*Obersturmführer* Franz Riedel, commander of 7 *Kompanie* 10 SS Pz Regt, recalls his orders:

'Attack Hill 113 at 0700 hours and following that Gavrus. Our forming-up zone was situated near Evrecy. My Kompanie should have been the point and 5 and 6 Kompanies were to be to the right and left rear. I was not informed of a postponement of the attack due to a delay in the arrival of the panzer grenadiers. Consequently, I launched my attack at the prescribed hour and my panzers rolled towards my objective. At the same time, an English armoured unit [44 RTR] with a great number of Shermans advanced across our front. In the blink of an eye, we fired and eleven of these Shermans burned on the hillside. My point tank commanded by Ewald Menzel destroyed five of the enemy tanks. We lost one tank... As the English were not able to reorganize after the shock of our surprise, we immediately advanced upon them and pursued by us, they rapidly retreated. Our pursuit would have been even more effective had the English not surrounded them selves by smoke. To follow them would have been fatal.

'At this point, I saw a motorcycle sidecar coming towards my tank containing commander II/10 SS Pz Regt, SS-Sturmbannführer Leo Rehinhold, who loudly demanded "What was the meaning of this farting about?" Then, as the smoke cleared, he saw the burning Shermans and his face lit up at the significance of my success. Hill 113 had been saved from the enemy'

44 RTR claimed that C Squadron lost three tanks on Hill 113, with two more badly damaged. It is also recorded that the casualties would have been heavier but for the fire of 4 Regiment Royal Horse Artillery. However, 29 Armoured Brigade noted in their war diary that the *'... regt [44 RTR], less one squadron attempted to outflank Esquay without success.'* Later a staff officer added:

'44 RTR sustained some tk cas during the morning from A-tk fire from high ground between Bourgy and Evrecy making progress on that flank expensive and the advance was halted.'

Elements of the *Hitlerjugend* and 88mm guns, in position on the southern slope of Hill 112, also played a part in stopping 44 RTR's advance. The RTR remained on the defensive in the western portion of the Odon Bridgehead for most of the day. The solo attack by the *Frundsberg's* 7 Panzer *Kompanie* showed the potential combat power that II SS *Panzerkorps* could apply in offensive operations.

Esquay Hill 113 le Bon Repos Gavrus

44 RTR

D8

The view west from Hill 112 across le Bon Repos to the open country 44 RTR crossed en route to Hill 113.

Hill 112

Although the panzers had halted 29 Armoured Brigade's advance short of Hill 113 and Esquay, II SS *Panzerkorps'* delayed counter-attack gave the British an opportunity to reoccupy Hill 112. 3 RTR, supported by two

In the foreground a crewman belonging to 44 RTR surveys the ground ahead. In the background a troop of Shermans including a Firefly wait to advance.

companies of 8 RB was ordered back to up to the crest of the feature. The tanks set off full of misgivings, anticipating another day under a continuous and heavy fire from the surrounding Germans. SS-*Standartenführer* Kurt Meyer wrote:

> *'Enemy artillery fire explored the ground around Verson. Shortly afterwards a massive barrage hit Hill 112. Would the British anticipate our plans and attack before we did? With an uncomfortable feeling, I watched tanks of 11th Armoured Division climb the slope south of the Odon and take Hill 112 in a pincer movement. The summit could no longer be identified. The impact of heavy gunfire was tossing the Norman soil around, metre by metre. There was no longer any doubt. The British had launched a pre-emptive attack. II SS Panzerkorps lost Hill 112.'*

It appears that in anticipation of II SS *Panzerkorps'* attack from the south west, Kurt Meyer's *Hitlerjugend* had erroniously relinquished responsibility for and its positions on Hill 112 shortly after dawn. However, with the delay in II SS *Panzerkorps'* attack, 3 RTR, taking advantage of another German staff error, 'surprisingly, reoccupied the hill with barely a shot being fired'. Hill 112 may have been occupied without loss but the Fife

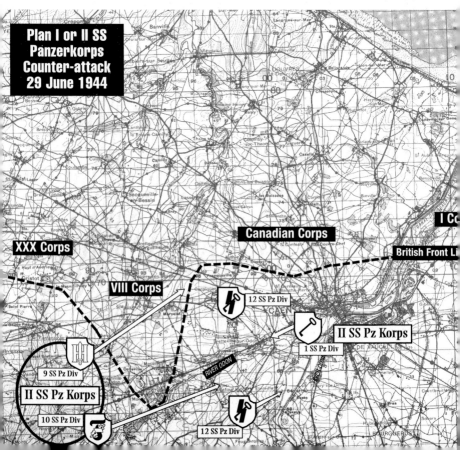

A panzer crew belonging to II Panzerkorps.

and Forfar Yeomanry were not so lucky. They were unable to make headway to the east of the feature, against 25 SS Pz Gr Regt who were well dug-in. On Hill 112, 3 RTR re-occupied its previous day's positions, on the northern slopes and taking advantage of the lack of defenders, advanced to the crest and occupied the wood and orchard around the spot height. However, as Major Noel Bell recalled, all was not quiet for long:

> *'Shelling and mortaring commenced, varying in pitch from time to time. Bren carriers were blown bodily off the ground, but there were no direct hits. Our mortars, working with those of 'H' Company, put down a steady stream of fire. Sergeant Hollands continued to operate the mortars until wounded by shrapnel. Naish, leaning against a bank above his slit trench, was holding the wireless headphones in his hand, the better to hear any approaching shells, when there was an explosion nearby; shrapnel tore through the Bakelite, leaving in his hand only the metal band.'*

Another description of the *Nebelwerfer* fire is recorded by Brigadier Essame:

> *'A howling and wailing grew until it filled the sky, rising in pitch as it approached, and ending in a series of shattering explosions all round us ... Then more squeals, the same horrible wail, and another batch of thirty-six bombs exploded astride us, so that the blast came first from one side, then from the other, then from both at once.'*

Withdrawal

Later in the morning, with the crisis approaching as II SS *Panzerkorps* concentrated on the tanks of the Scottish Corridor, the British were under pressure. In Montgomery's words:

> *'In view of this it was decided that VIII Corps should concentrate for the time being on holding the ground won, and regrouping started with the object of withdrawing the armour into reserve ready for new thrusts.'*

This decision in fact resulted, from confirmation of ULTRA interceptions and decryptions of German radio orders that had been in the hands of Generals Montgomery and Dempsey for several days. They knew that II SS *Panzerkorps'* intentions were 'to take the Baron, Mouen, Cheux area and to destroy the enemy who has advanced across the Caen – Villiers-Bocage road'.

Armed with this outline information, according to the VIII Corps' History:

> *'At 1000 hours General O'Connor held a conference at Headquarters 15 (Scottish) Division in which he announced that in view of the general situation any further advance to the Orne would be temporally stopped, and present positions maintained. A general consolidation would take place with particular stress on the co-ordination of anti-tank defence, and the positioning of the armoured brigades. Certain re-grouping too, on account... of intermingling of units. Areas of responsibility were re-assigned and every effort was made to 'tidy up' the sector in order to take the shock of what had every appearance of becoming the first major enemy offensive since the Allies had landed.'*

On Hill 112, Trooper John Thorpe, of 3 RTR, recorded in his diary:

> *'Warning Order received: Abandon tanks after destroying the gun. But no action until confirmed. New orders: Retreat, taking the tanks with us. Does anyone know what is going on?'*

Despite the confusion, 29 Brigade was eventually ordered to abandon Hill 112. With two fresh SS panzer divisions approaching from the west, British commanders feared that its defenders, exposed at the end of the Scottish Corridor, could not hold the hill. In addition, the tanks of 11th Armoured Division, were urgently needed to hold the Corridor north of the Odon and 15th Scottish and 43rd Wessex Divisions were already fully committed to holding ground. With the gift of hindsight, it is clear that British commanders had failed to fully appreciated the operational value of Hill 112 and had overestimated the power of II SS *Panzerkorps* when faced with the overwhelming Allied air and artillery fire support. South of the Odon, British commanders were content to hold a shallow bridgehead and give

Knocked out Shermans on the slope of Hill 112.

up the firm hold they had on Hill 112. The battle resulting from, this decision was to have tragic consequences for many of the soldiers who were to fight on the slopes of Hill 112 over the following seven weeks.

II SS *Panzerkorps'* Counter-Attack

With the traffic jams in the Scottish Corridor worse than ever and as the British regrouped, the Germans were facing a different problem. The sun had broken through the glowering skies of the previous days enabling the Allied airforces to be unleashed. From dawn onwards, air recce reports had been flowing into British Headquarters that there was large-scale eastward movement from Flers northwards to Argentan and Vire. Most of the traffic identified by the Allied airmen was the Germans' tail of logistic vehicles, heading towards a triangle of ground between the villages of Evrecy, Noyers and Villers-Bocage. Armed with visual confirmation of II SS *Panzerkorps'* concentration area, General Dempsey was able to act on the ULTRA information already in his hands.

In response to Germans preparations to mount their first significant counter-stroke since D-Day, the British concentrated their firepower to reduce the combat effectiveness of II SS *Panzerkorps* before it could come into contact. Allied fighter-bombers were promptly in action, claiming to have destroyed or damaged a hundred German transport vehicles and heavy artillery and naval gunfire also joined the deep battle. VIII Corps recorded:

> *'Whilst the RAF was attacking the enemy moving up from the south, the Corps artillery, fed with unusually plentiful information from its Air OPs and counter battery sources, fired heavy concentrations on likely enemy assembly areas and forming up places, in addition to giving maximum aid to the forward troops in response to an increasingly large number of calls for direct support from them.'*

Early casualties resulting from the Allied air and deep artillery strikes included seven precious fuel bowsers.

Veterans of the Eastern Front, 9th *Hoenstaufen* and 10th *Frundsberg* SS Panzer Divisions were used to artillery concentrations but nothing had prepared them for the neutralizing effect of the Allied firepower that they were now experiencing. A translation of an unfinished letter, written by an SS *Rottenführer* of 10th SS Panzer Division taken prisoner on 30 June, was published in a Second Army intelligence summary:

> *'We are now 30 kilometres behind the front after a nightmare journey across France, which has taken a fortnight under the most frightening conditions on account of the enemy planes. For the last fortnight I have hardly slept at all and have forgotten how many times the enemy has straffed us. We have suffered many casualties in men and vehicles, but our so-called Luftwaffe has not ventured to put in an appearance. There was nothing like this in Russia, and we are all wondering whether life at the front will be as bad.'*

German troops had to be constantly on the alert for 'Jabos'.

It was, and he went on to say:

> *'Before dawn we took up sheltered positions in a wood and took some sleep. After only a short time, it was light and we were under fire of very heavy guns. We are now sheltering in our panzers, which are being shaken to pieces by blast and shell splinters.'*

VIII Corps' intelligence summary, under the air paragraph also describes how: 'The fighter bomber pilots had a very happy time with a concentration of tanks discovered near Villers-Bocage'. Particularly badly hit by air strikes was a *kampfgruppe* consisting of III/20 SS Pz Gr Regt and the Panthers of I/9 SS Panzer Regt, who moving forward from Villers Bocage to their assembly area at Bas des Forges. Due to deliver a crushing assault on Cheux, they were attacked by an estimated one hundred Lancaster bombers. SS-*Mann*

Typhoons loaded with bombs and rockets made movement by road and manoeuvre on the field of battle a highly risky business for the Germans. Luftwaffe fighters were absent from the skies over Normandy.

Armoured vehicles belonging to Das Reich, having been hit by concentrated Typhoon attack.

Wilhelm Tieke was on the receiving end:

> *'The bombs rained down. They tore at the earth. They snapped the tree trunks like matchsticks, threw armoured vehicles into the air, ripped off their tracks and even armour plate.'*

In this *Kampfgruppen* twenty men were killed and forty wounded. Eighty percent of the armoured vehicles were damaged in some way. Also hit in the raids, was the *Hohenstaufen's* tactical headquarters at les Nouillons.

H-Hour for II SS *Panzerkorps'* attack, at 0700 hours, was initially delayed for two hours and later in the morning, SS-*Gruppenführer* Bittrich signalled

The main gun of the Army Group Royal Artillery was the 5.5 inch gun.

Panzergruppen West that:

> '*The offensive can not begin until the afternoon. Our concentrations are under continual artillery and air bombardment'.*

Another message at 1340 hours excused an even longer delay:

> '*The enemy fighter bomber attacks are causing heavy loses... and the panzer divisions can not bring their tanks forward due to a lack of fuel.'*

The attack, according to German war diaries, eventually started at between 1430 and 1530 hours. SS-*Obergruppenführer* Hauser also reported that: 'This great artillery fire is taking its toll on morale'.

Most German commanders believe that II SS *Panzerkorp's* counter-stroke had failed before it began. However, it is considered that the physical destruction caused by the British land, sea and air bombardment was greatly overstated, in order to excuse failure. Nevertheless, the British artillery and air strikes did neutralise the German attack for some hours, by causing damage, preventing essential preparations and orders being issued. Consequently, time was gained for units of VIII Corps to redeploy and improve their positions. The delay also permitted 43rd Wessex Division to attack the Mouen area, which effectively spoiled the supporting attack that the *Leibstandarte* was planned to deliver. Overall, the German attack was blunted by the air and artillery strikes but not stopped.

Despite the delays, SS-*Obergruppenführer* Bittrich's plans for II SS *Panzerkorps*, with over four hundred panzers and *sturmguschutz*, were unchanged. He planned to attack with his two SS panzer divisions from the **See maps pages 155 and 161** west, astride the Odon. 9th *Hohenstaufen* were to attack to the north of the river valley and 10th *Frundsberg* to the south. The *Hohenstaufen's* mission was to cut the Corridor (*Korp's* main effort) and reach the *Hitlerjugend's* positions on Carpiquet Airfield, while the *Frundsberg* was to destroy the enemy on Hill 112 and in the Tourmauville bridgehead south of the Odon. The *Hitlerjugend* were to support the *Leibstandarte's* attack on the Allied salient from the south east but otherwise remain on the defensive.

The *Hohenstaufen's* Attack North of the Odon

SS-*Standartenführer* Thomas Muller's plan for 9th SS Panzer Division was to advance eastwards to their objective on a line between Cheux and Mouen. *Kampfgruppe* Weidinger, under command from 2nd *Das Reich* SS Panzer Division was to support the attack on the left flank. Cheux was identified as key terrain in the coming battle, because seizing the village would cut the salient that VIII Corps had driven into the German line.

The *Hohenstaufen's* preparations for the attack were not only disrupted by air and artillery strikes but also by an attack by 8 Royal Scots, which was mounted to improve their positions in the woods around Chateau Grainville. In doing so, 8 RS engaged with direct fire and with artillery on likely enemy depth positions. These targets included les Nouillons Farm

159

Hill 112

Gavrus

Hill 113

Odon Valle

The view from Grainville looking south across the Odon to Gavrus and the open ground on Hill 113 beyond.

where Tactical HQ, 9th SS *Panzer* Division was setting up during the early stage of their attack. SS-*Mann* Georg Essler, a Mark IV driver in 9 SS Pz Regt, recalled the opening stage of his first battle in the west:

> *'... we boarded our vehicles and followed a guide to a new attack point. A great battle was in progress, we saw a lot of smoke, and overhead the Allied planes were making constant attacks on our forces. Some of our comrades were already engaged elsewhere, and we received an order to go in and crush the British Salient. We went across the fields with our infantry and at once came under very heavy artillery fire, which disrupted everything.'*

The *Hohenstaufen's* attack was mounted from the Noyers / Haut des Forges / Vendes area, across the southern end of the Rauray Spur using the road

Looking north to Grainville and le Valtru.

A Scottish lance corporal firing from the cover of a hedgerow.

towards Cheux as the axis. However, the Germans concluded, as had VIII Corps, that the dominating Rauray Spur needed to be recaptured before an attack on Cheux could succeed. Therefore, the first objective was the village of Rauray, to the left of the axis, which *Kampfgruppe* Weidinger attacked from its existing positions around in Brettevillette.

Facing Weidinger, whose attack started earlier than the main assault, was 70 Brigade of 49th Division. As has already been noted, Rauray had been taken by 11 DLI on 27 June and on 28 June, 10 DLI had occupied Point 110 on the crest of the Rauray Spur to the south of the village. Forewarned of the German attack, the 49th's proposed attack on Brettvillette was postponed and the infantry set about improving their defences. Consequently, when their blow fell

SS-Obersturmbannführer Otto Weidinger.

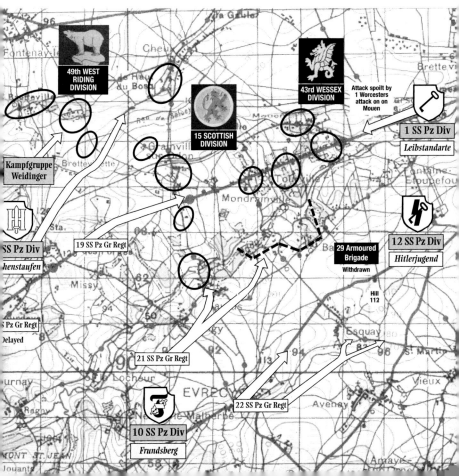

Armoured half tracks carried the 3rd Battalions of SS Panzer Grenadier Regiments into action. The vehicle on the left is a command variant.

from the south west, *Kampfgruppe* Weidinger was repulsed.

The *Hohenstaufen's* main effort was III/19 SS Pz Grs, mounted in half-tracks, they were to advance north east astride the Noyers - Cheux road. Supporting the panzer grenadier's attack was a *kompanie* of Panthers from I/9 SS Pz Regt. The *Kampfgruppe* crossed the top of the Rauray Spur and started to descend into a shallow valley of small, thickly hedged fields.

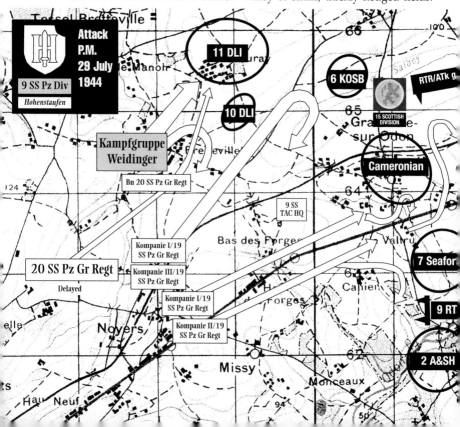

Now in full view of the dug-in British infantry, the Germans came under anti-tank fire from guns in well co-ordinated positions that covered all approaches. The SS infantry debussed from their half-tracks and took cover in the hedgerows, while the Panthers moved into covered fire positions, from where their superior, high velocity, 75mm guns knocked out counter-attacking British tanks.

Meanwhile in the 'British salient', 4 Dorsets were moving up to reinforce the Scottish Corridor. The Battalion's Signal Platoon Sergeant recalled that at 1500 hours:

'We were travelling through the gun areas when we were ordered to halt and disperse, everyone wondered what was happening, suddenly we were shaken by a thundering roar, every gun in the area opened up. What a barrage, red flames and puffs of smoke from cleverly concealed guns could be seen clearly, rapid fire seemed to work like clockwork. We couldn't hear our selves speak. Officers and NCOs, including myself, shouted to the men, at the top of our voices; telling them to disperse and take up emergency positions, as we were informed that Jerry was putting in a strong counter attack.'

For the second time during the day, an artillery hammer blow struck II SS *Panzerkorps*. III/19 SS Pz Gr's attack came to an abrupt halt, forming a small salient sandwiched between 44 (Lowland) Brigade in Grainville and the leading elements of 49th West Riding Division on the Rauray Spur. A thousand yards short of le Haut du Bosq, the *Hohenstaufen's* main effort had failed. They would have to fight to clear their flanks if they were to resume their advance and take Cheux.

Facing the *Hohenstaufen's* second southerly axis, 8 RS were reorganizing having taken Chateau Grainville, when they were attacked by I and II/19 SS Pz Gr Regt. According to the divisional historian 'they were pushed out of it by an immediate counter-attack. Back they came again and retook the wood, thereafter they held their front despite severe enemy pressure.'

BBC corespondent Chester Wilmot, recorded a report describing the attack at Grainville.

'The Germans attacked twice, first at two thirty in the afternoon, and for more than an hour there was a tank and infantry melee, concentrated mainly around the [Grainville] Chateau, where our troops were established in orchards and gardens. The Germans sent flame-throwers as well as tanks to support their infantry. The enemy

Chateau Granville.

**Armoured battalion panzer grenadiers in their well camouflaged
half-tracks.**

infantry were pinned down in long grass, short of one company position. Two flame-throwers under covering fire from heavy German tanks that lay hidden in the hedges moved up. The flame-throwers got close enough to spray the very trenches from which the Scotsmen were fighting. Flames licked the hedges, and burnt up the grass around them, but the men kept their heads down and struck to their positions. ...and while they held their ground, Churchill tanks, hidden in hedges behind them, drove off the flame-throwers and the tanks. The German attack petered out, but it cost them five Panthers which were knocked out by the Churchills and our anti-tank guns.'

8 RS and 9 Cameronian, supported by 9 RTR holding the Grainville area, had also suffered heavily but a war corespondent of the day could not report this. Nor could he mention that panzer grenadiers had in fact, at one point, pushed the Cameronians back almost as far as the railway line.

At 1600 hours, 8 RS captured an officer from 19 SS Pz Gr Regt in the northern outskirts of Grainville, confirming that 9th SS *Hohenstaufen* was the formation attacking the Corridor north of the Odon. His marked map and note book confirmed the detail of II SS *Panzerkorps'* aims that intelligence staffs had already developed. However, such information in a midst of a battle is difficult to exploit, as the troops were already locked in combat.

Meanwhile, 20 SS Pz Gr Regt struggled to free itself from the chaos in the assembly area and only took part in the closing stages of the attack. The three panzer grenadier battalions were thrown into battle piecemeal as they arrived, reinforcing 19 SS Pz Grs. One of the battalions succeeded in securing a foothold in Rauray and on the Spur, having attacked from the south. However, this hold on Rauray proved to be temporary, as only a small force had reach the village.

Back at Chateau Grainville, 8 RS, who had suffered heavy casualties holding their positions, were to be relieved by 6 Royal Scots Fusiliers at 1700 hours. However, at 1830 hours, according to the Scots' divisional historian:

'As this relief was in progress the enemy put in a particularly heavy counter-attack, which caught the forward companies on the wrong foot. First, enemy tanks lay off hull-down and picked off the Royal Scot's forward A-Tk guns. Then two flame-throwing tanks charged home into the two forward company areas, where they milled round and killed a lot of men in a particularly unpleasant manner before they withdrew.

'For a time there was great confusion. Profiting by this, a number of enemy tanks penetrated deeply into our forward positions. Enemy infantry was following. It was a very critical moment... Responding magnificently, our infantry counter-attacked in their turn and halted

the enemy infantry thus depriving the enemy tanks of their infantry support.'

Now, unsupported by infantry, the Mark IVs of 7 Panzer *Kompanie*, taking a southerly route via le Valtru, broke through between Grainville and Collville. Advancing from the south towards Cheux, the panzers were halted by the 17-pounder M10s belonging to a battery from 91 Anti-Tank Regiment and the Shermans of 4 Armoured Brigade, deployed as a 'back stop' to 15th Scottish. Deep in the hull of one of the Mark IVs was SS-*Mann* Essler, who continued his account:

'There was so much smoke I could hardly see, and I thought it very dangerous if we lost touch with our infantry. Then my commander, who was a Unterscharführer, *told us there were enemy tanks ahead, so we opened fire at once. The bangs were continuous and I could hardly see a thing. Then I was ordered to stop while our gunner shot up some enemy tanks and other vehicles. And then we received a hit on the front of our panzer, which shook us up a bit, but did no real damage. We changed our position and I found I could see the enemy tanks ahead quite clearly in another field, and they were shooting at us. We found a little dip from where we could shoot many targets from a covered hull-down position. Then came a series of loud explosions around the panzer and we realized we were under artillery fire. So we withdrew, but we were on open ground and still under heavy fire, so I reversed again and saw one of our panzers burst into flames and two men jumping out. It was all very terrifying.*

'Our gunner found that he could no longer traverse the turret, so I turned the tank so he could lay the gun and we hit several more enemy tanks and vehicles.

'Then something hit us very hard in the flank and we smelt burning. The Unterscharführer *ordered us out quick, so I tried to unfasten my front hatch, but it was jammed. By the time I scrambled up into the turret, the whole panzer was on fire and my clothing was smoking. I just managed to jump onto the grass when it went up and the ammunition began to explode.'*

As dusk approached, the *Hohenstaufen* was a spent force. They had been beaten back from Cheux and abandoning their footholds in and around Rauray and Grainville, they broke contact with the Scots and withdrew to their start lines.

The *Frundsberg's* Attack South of the Odon

South of the Odon, 11th Armoured Division had started the day attempting to expand its bridged to the south and to the west, with 44

(Lowland) Brigade being tasked to 'tidy up' the western flank. They were unable to complete this task, leaving 2 A&SH almost isolated, at the Gavrus Bridges. However, 29 Armoured Brigade had sent infantry patrols from 8 Rifle Brigade, supported by a troop of Shermans to reoccupy Gavrus in order to bolster this exposed flank.

Meanwhile, having shaken themselves free of the chaos in their assembly area, 21 SS Pz Gr Regt prepared to lead the *Frundsberg's* attack. Their mission was to destroy VIII Corps' bridgehead and recapture the Odon Bridges at Gavrus and Tourmauville in order to establish lateral routes north to the *Hohenstaufen*. They formed up in the woods west of Bougy and in the first phase of the attack, they advanced eastwards. At 1550 hours, Headquarters 29 Armoured Brigade was reporting that 'Gavrus is being attacked by tks and inf'. The panzer grenadiers described resulting fighting against 8 RB's patrols as 'fierce'. However, after almost two hours of combat, 21 SS Pz Gr Regt had fought through Gavrus pushing the British back into the valley. At 1740 hours, 11th Armoured Division's

See map page 161

A well camouflaged Panzer MkIV hoping for concealment from both ground and air observers.

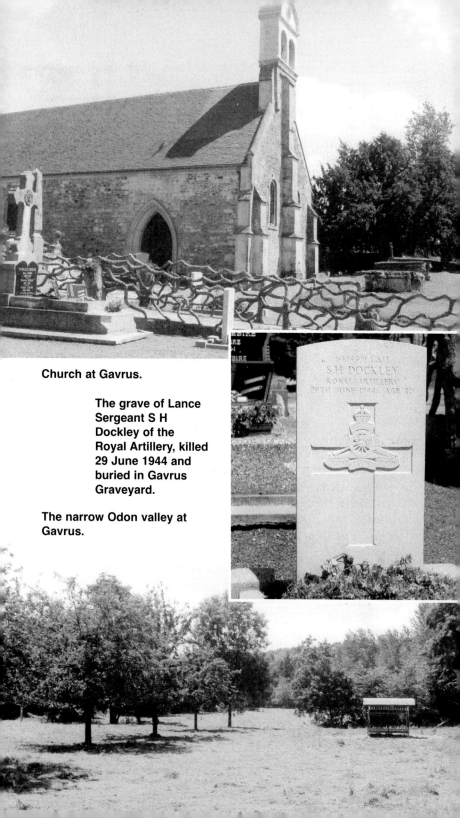

Church at Gavrus.

The grave of Lance Sergeant S H Dockley of the Royal Artillery, killed 29 June 1944 and buried in Gavrus Graveyard.

The narrow Odon valley at Gavrus.

The double bridges at Gavrus held by 2 A&SH. Looking south on the D139.

war diary record '29 Armd Bde report having to pull out of Gavrus', With the village clear, the Germans continued their advance. Almost immediately, the *kampfgruppen* heading north to the Odon, ran into 2 A&SH, who was still dug-in in close defence of the bridges. The artillery again helped blunt the German attack, while the Argyles' 6-pounder anti-tank guns, engaged targets at short range and the Royal Artillery 17-pounders, covered the open ground and longer fields of fire. Battalion anti-tank gunner Corporal Campbell recorded:

> 'All sort of reports were coming in about a big attack and we came under more and more fire. We were told by the CO to burn all our personal things except our pay books, as we were surrounded. It wasn't a pleasant feeling to have tanks behind us. The Seaforth did a splendid job in stopping them totally cutting us of but we sent a day and a half with Germans all around us. At night time we were kept awake by German machine guns firing tracer on fixed lines.'

After four hours of determined attacks, the panzer grenadiers were beaten off and the Argyles stubornly held onto the important bridges.

Meanwhile, the remainder of 21 SS Pz Gr Regt, supported by the *Sturmguschutz* of 10 SS *Panzerjäger* Battalion, continued the advance east towards the Tourmauville Bridgehead. Here, at 1755 hours: '159 Brigade report enemy infiltrating into 1 HEREFORD posn' and five minutes later 'that the RIGHT Coy of 1 HEREFORD overrun'. However, the German attack was running out of steam, as illustrated by the following two entries in 11th Armoured Division's war diary entries:

169

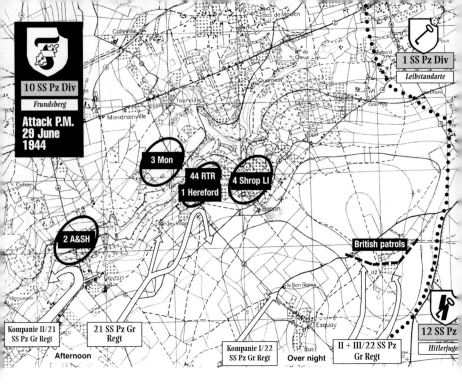

'1815 hrs. Enemy attack on 1 HEREFORD held and enemy starting withdrawing. 29 Armd Bde report enemy having brought up some SP guns under cover of woods in area of Gavrus, which succeeded in inflicting hy cas on one sqn of 44 RTR.

'1830 hrs. 159 Inf report spasmodic automatic fire in woods to the NORTH of the river. Situation well under control.'

The part played by the artillery in preventing the *Frundsberg* from pressing home their attack can not be over estimated. Major Steel Brownlie wrote of the Ayrshire Yeomanry Field Regiment:

'Captain Walton with the Herefords reported a developing enemy attack, and a fire plan was arranged by Colonel Phillips and the commander of 159 Infantry Brigade. The entire artillery of 11th Armoured Division, 15th (Scottish) Division and 8th AGRA fired, the Yeomanry expending 90 rounds per gun in two hours. The attack was broken, and Captain Walton and Captain Garrett remained in observation to engage casual targets.'

Four hours after crossing its start line, 21 SS Pz Gr withdrew.

Night Attack 29/30 June 1944

As the German attack slackened, General O'Connor's orders for the redeployment of his armour to north of the Odon were being completed.

170

SS Panzer grenadiers supported by Panthers advance to contact through Brettvillette on the afternoon of 29 June 1944.

SS Panzer grenadiers advancing through waist high corn.

British artillery helped stop the attack by the Frundsberg.

In expectation of a renewed attack by II SS *Panzerkorps*, General O'Connor had positioned Churchills of 31 Tank Brigade in support the infantry and anti-tank guns in a screen in depth along the Corridor. 4 and 29 Armoured Brigades were concentrating in positions around Norrey-en-Bessin. From these assembly areas, they were to be prepared to counter-attack the flank of any German penetration of the infantry positions. However, for the armoured brigades, there followed a long and chaotic night of renewed traffic jams on the cleared routes back towards Norrey.

HQ *Panzergruppe* West was not, however, content to let the attacks peter out. II SS *Panzerkorps* was ordered to renew the attack under cover of darkness. It was reasoned that, at night, without being subject to air attack and with Allied artillery observation less than fully effective, the panzer grenadiers would not be under the same disadvantage as they had been during daylight. According to *Panzergruppe* West's war diary, Rommel gave his thoughts to Bittrich over the telephone:

> 'The II SS Panzerkorps *counter-attack presents the big opportunity. The* Schwerepunkt *is to be kept on the left with Cheux as the main objective.'*

Again, the *Hohenstaufen* were to be the main effort for the night attack. Their plan was almost exactly the same as it had been earlier in the day; an attack towards Cheux and the Carpiquet area beyond. The advancing panzers ran into a screen of recce Cromwells deployed by 2 Northamptonshire Yeomanry, who had been earlier sent forward to sweep the area of the afternoon's attack. The Yeomanry's screen having fallen back, the artillery and anti-tank guns engaged the panzers under the flickering light of star shells and again halted them.

To the south of the river, the *Frundsberg's* advance progressed well and by 0400 hours, SS-*Standartenführer* Deisenhofer's 21 SS Pz Gr Regt was closing in on the Tourmauville Bridge, still held by 1 Hereford, and had again virtually isolated the Argyles at the Gavrus Bridges. However, the attack was halted by artillery that produced 'a wall of protective fire' around the bridgehead. The British artillery tactics were pragmatic. Rather than attempting to strike individual German units moving somewhere in the darkness they resorted to firing protective barrages. Further south SS-*Sturmbannführer* Schulze's 22 SS Pz Gr Regt, who had not been committed during the earlier attack, moved to secure the Hill 112 area to prevent its seizure if the British renewed their advance. I/Battalion advanced east on the Evrecy – Caen Road to le Bon Repos without opposition. Here it dug-in under artillery fire, which caused some casualties. To the south of Hill 112, II and III/Battalions pressed forward onto the slopes of the feature and took over the *Hitlerjugend's* re-established but worn out and thinly spread defences. Even if General O'Connor could or had wished to resume the advance to the Orne, any chance had passed, now that 10th SS Panzer Division surrounded Hill 112 in strength.

Summary

After the war, SS-*Obergruppenführer* Hausser, commander II *Panzerkorps*, told his Intelligence Corps debriefer about the main features of the fighting on 29 June:

> *'It was scheduled to begin at seven o'clock in the morning, but hardly had the tanks assembled when they were attacked by fighter-bombers. This disrupted the troops so much that the attack did not start again until two-thirty in the afternoon. But even then it could not get*

SS Panzer grenadiers take a smoking break.

going. The murderous fire from naval guns in the Channel and the terrible British artillery destroyed the bulk of our attacking force in its assembly area. The few tanks that did manage to go forward were easily stopped by the British anti-tank gunners. In my opinion, the attack was prepared too quickly. I wanted to wait another two days but Hitler insisted that it be launched on 29 June.'

Hausser was not to know that more time would have made little difference, as his intentions had been fully revealed by ULTRA decryptions of his radio traffic. The fully concentrated II SS *Panzerkorps* would still have been struck and badly written down by a massive Allied air and artillery attack.

Before the invasion *Feldmarschall* Rommel had predicted that the Germans would be unable to effectively concentrate panzer formations and launch them into battle under the gaze of Allied airmen. The firepower concentrated against II SS *Panzerkorps* on 29 June 1944, in the form of Allied bombers, fighters and fighter-bombers, coupled with British artillery and naval gunfire support arguably proved him to be correct.

The morale of II SS *Panzerkorps*, however, remained high. Surly, confident, SS soldiers taken prisoner:

'...assured their captors that the boot would soon be on the other foot, as they had a "pep talk" in which they had been assured that London had been destroyed by V1s and twelve million Britons were dead.'

SS prisoners from II SS Panzerkorps. Most were confident that their captivity would be brief.

CHAPTER SEVEN

Epilogue

In response to the threat posed by II SS *Panzerkorps*, General Dempsey ordered extensive, operational level, regrouping, which came into effect at midnight 29/30 June. The following key formations and units were amongst those moving overnight to reinforce the Scottish Corridor: 53rd Welsh Division and 86 Anti-Tank Regiment, from XII Corps and 68 Medium Regiment RA from I Corps. The British offensive was at an end but German commanders harboured a desire to destroy the dangerous salient.

North of the Odon, with 29 and 4 Armoured Brigades' traffic jams cleared, they completed their slow move to positions to the north and began the process of replenishing and repairing the tanks. Meanwhile commanders received orders and examined potential counter-attack options. In the front line, Scottish and Westcountry infantry endured rain and shelling. Brigadier Essame recalled that a:

> '... *heavy and continuous mortar and artillery fire rained down on the track and the houses and orchards of Tourville, Mondrainville and Mouen. Around the bottleneck by the church in Tourville, buildings were in flames. The woods along the Odon and the main road remained under concentrated bombardment all day. Casualties began to pile up. Much of the fire came from a Werfer regiment to the south of Hill 112.'*

However, the Brigadier continued to say that the shelling and mortaring was not all one way and that a considerable artillery duel was fought.

With the enemy pushed back, envious British tanks crews from British armoured regiments examine Tigers and Panthers – what chance against these.

> *'Meanwhile, 94, 112 and 179 Field Regiments hit back, firing battery, regimental and even Corps targets all day. The 4.2s of 8 Middlesex came into action side by side with the infantry. The 3-in mortars of the forward battalions opened up. Even captured mortars were pressed into service.'*

On top of the fire of the divisional artillery, Brigadier Churcher calculated that the guns of 8 AGRA fired approximately 38,000 rounds in the reporting period 30/31 June 1944. It is the use of quantities of ammunition such as this which contributed to the daily casualty rates in Normandy typically exceeding those of Passchendaele during the Great War.

It was not just an artillery duel that prompted this expenditure of ammunition but a series of German attacks. The corps historian recorded recorded:

> *'The enemy was doubtless licking his wounds and regrouping his units after the terrible losses of the previous day. At all events no major effort was developed against 8 Corps during the whole of 30 June, though its opponents remained active and launched several probing attacks on a small scale. Thus at 1150 hours, 159 Infantry Brigade and 2 Argyles* [in the western portion of the Odon Bridgehead] *repulsed two companies of panzer grenadiers supported by tanks coming from the direction of Esquay, whilst in the middle of the afternoon the enemy tried again in a different sector – that held by 46 (Highland) Brigade* [in the Grainville area], *and for a short while succeeded in penetrating its southern positions. Within the hour, however, 7 Seaforth Highlanders had effectively dealt with this attempt.'*

However, with the Argyles under sustained pressure Brigadier Makintosh-Walker ordered the abandonment of the positions that they had gallantly held for three days around the Gavrus Bridges. Having repelled successive counterattacks,

> *'At 9.30 PM Major McElwee, now the Senior officer present, withdrew the three companies across both bridges without further loss and took them back by way of le Valtru – where the Seaforth were busy repelling a counter-attack – and Mondrainville to Colleville, where they found the headquarters of 227th Brigade.*

> *'Gavrus alone had been lost. For the rest, at the close of the fighting on 30 June the Division held all its positions firmly.'*

The day ended with a controversial air raid by 250 Lancasters, who dropped 1,253 tons of bombs on the German transport bottleneck at Villers-Bocage. The town was largely destroyed and became a 'no go area' as the raid had included bombs with delay fuses set for up to thirty-six hours.

Over the period 31 June to 2 July, 53rd Welsh Division took over the

British soldiers inspect a Panzer MkIV. It appears to have lost a track whilst withdrawing; the turret has been turned to the rear.

western flank of the Scottish Corridor. To the east of the Odon Bridgehead, 43rd (Wessex) Division continued to fight along the valley from Baron towards Verson, overlooked during the succeeding days, by 10th *Frundsberg* SS Panzer Division who developed strong defensive positions on Hill 112. While not producing the same level of casualties as full offensive battle conditions, both sides suffered a steady stream of casualties. For the British, the Odon Valley became known as Death Valley, which subject to German harassing fire had to be negotiated in order to reach forward positions in the bridgehead. Eventually the Wessex Division cleared the *Leibstandarte* from the Odon Valley as far east as Verson.

Fighting continued over the next nine days, with the British divisions mounting a series of attacks so as to improve their positions astride the Odon Valley and the German mounting further battalion level counter-attacks. With VIII Corps concentrating on holding positions gained during EPSOM, Second Army's main effort fell initially to the Canadians who eventually took the heavily defended Carpiquet Airfield from the *Hitlerjugend*. Following the clearance of the airfield on the high ground immediately west of the city, I Corps, with Bomber Command support, fought their way into Caen from the north and finally secured their D-Day objective on 9 July 1944.

Following the liberation of Caen there followed the epic battle fought by the Wessex Division to recapture Hill 112 in Operation JUPITER. The Westcountrymen captured the northern slopes of the hill and drove the Germans off the crest line. It became a no-man's-land that held many characteristics of the Great War. The protracted battle for what is now quiet open farmland, went on until 23 August 1944 and is fully covered in the *Battleground Europe* title **Hill 112**.

The American General Omar Bradley summed up the strategic

background to EPSOM and its aftermath:

'*The containment mission that had been assigned Monty was not calculated to burnish British pride in the accomplishment of their troops. For in the minds of most people, success in battle is measured in the rate and length of advance. They found it difficult to realize that the more successful Monty was in stirring up German resistance, the less likely he was to advance. By the end of June, Rommel had concentrated seven panzer divisions against Monty's British Sector. One was all the enemy could spare for the US front.*'

Chapter Eight

EPSOM Tour Directions

From Caen and the east – From the Caen *Peripherique* take the **N13** towards Cherbourg. After two miles, take the **Rots** turning onto **D86c**. Drive through Rots to **Bretville 'Orgueilleuse**.

From Bayeux – on the **N13** towards Caen, take the turning signposted to **Bretville 'Orgueilleuse**. Go through the **N13** underpass (4 metre coach clearance) and turn right on the **D83c** towards Bretteville and Rots.

In the centre of Bretville l'Orgueilleuse **turn at the traffic lights by the church** onto the D83 towards **St Manvieu-Norrey**. Go through the underpass (the only full height crossing of the N13 in the area) and continue across the railway bridge ❶ towards Manvieu-Norrey. The railway line was the EPSOM start line. This is the area across which 44 Lowland Brigade advanced to reach St Manvieu. 6 RSF were on the left and 8 RS on the right south of Norrey. Good views from the bridge.

Follow the D83 around an S bend by a wood. **Turn into a lay-by / junction on the left** (on to a farm track) and park safely off the road ❷. From here, there are excellent views across the fields of the broad Mue valley unchanged since 1944. Note the tower blocks of Caen on the eastern horizon and just to the west of the city the half moon shapes of the Carpiquet Airfield hangers which were strongly held by 25 Regt *Hitlerjugend*. In the trees to the south, is the village of St Manvieu, which was held by 1/26 Pz Gr Regt. Looking west is the open area held by 12 SS Pioneers and the church tower of Norrey-en-Bessin.

Drive on down into the Mue valley and at the edge of the village of **St Manvieux** turn off the D 83 onto the D147A. The insignificant bridge by the village sign crosses the Mue, ❸ which is dry for most of the year. Drive through the new part of the village. Following the *l'Affrondement* sign, turn right. The SS panzer grenadiers converted the old, stout farm buildings in this part of the village into strong points. Park by the blue **NTL totem** ❹ in the small square in front of the church. The church, as was much of the village centre, was totally destroyed during the EPSOM fighting and the following weeks of July 1944. Continue out of the village. **Turn right** onto the **D9** towards **Fontenay-le-Pesnel**.

Ignoring the turnings to Cheux (pronounced Sher), park in the lay-by adjacent to the entrance to the **St Manvieux Commonwealth War Graves Commission Cemetery**. ❺ This is a large post-war concentration cemetery, containing 2,183 graves. A significant proportion of the dead buried here belongs to the EPSOM period. Immediately inside the entrance is a row of 10 HLI graves all dated 27 June. These soldiers were killed in the Battalion's renewed attacks south of Cheux. There are two sizeable plots of German graves. The German headstones are without ranks but, despite the lack of rank, the ages and dates of death indicate that a significant proportion belong to the *Hitlerjugend*. Return to your car.

Take the turning to **Cheux** (D83) nearest to the cemetery. This was the main route forward for two whole divisions, until the engineers had cleared and marked the routes 'Moon' and 'Star' across country. The road through the village ❻ was choked with rubble and swept by rifle fire and mortar fire. As the volume of traffic attempting to reach the front increased and the heavy rain continued, the roads became reduced to large muddy puddles. The deadly chaos in Cheux is easily imagined.

Continue south through the rebuilt village of Cheux. Drive past a couple of paddocks and a water tower on the left. Immediately after a large stone farm, turn right onto **Rue des Raux** and park. ❼ This is the area, le Haut du Bosqu, 5 DCLI was occupying when Panthers of 2nd *Wien* Panzer Division came down the road from the west and entered the orchard alongside the barn where Battalion HQ was setting up. Here the Cornishmen knocked out five of the unsupported Panthers during a close quarter battle.

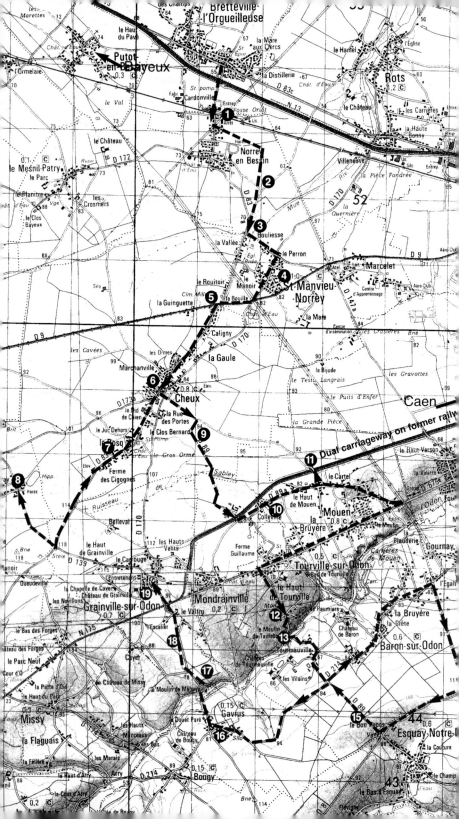

Drive on south on the D83. As the road rises through the hedgerows, the area where 10 HLI fought its battles against SS-*Hauptsturmführer* Seigle's panzers and assorted panzer grenadiers on the afternoon of 26 June and the morning of 27 June. Continue on to a crossroads. Turn right on to the D139 towards **Rauray** and **Fontenay-le-Pesnel**. Drive across the plateau of the Rauay Spur to the village of Rauay. At the northern edge of the village, **take a right turn** onto a minor road. From here ❽ the view to the north east, across the EPSOM battle area, underlines the tactical importance of the feature. With the Rauray Spur in German hands, 15th Scottish Division's advance was always going to be difficult.

Retrace the route back to Cheux. At the cross roads in the centre of the village, near the church, turn right onto the **D 89** towards **Colleville and Tourville**. Emerging into open country, the visitor is on the broad open plateau of Ring Contour 100 ❾. To the north, British armour congregated in the dead ground, while on the plateau itself, burnt out wrecks littered the ground. To the south, German panzers and anti-tank guns were positioned on the ridge, engaging any vehicle showing itself on Ring Contour 100. The infantry of 2 A&SH eventually forced the position. Drive on down across the Sabley stream and across the main road, which was a railwayline in 1944. Across the main road / railway, turn left onto the D89A through Colleville ❿ towards Mouen. Following the Argyles into Colleville, was 10 HLI which attacked the *Leibstandarte* in Mouen on 29 June. Driving into Mouen, turn left and drive across the road bridge and park ⓫ Looking north across the open fields, is the ground across which 1 Worcesters delivered their successful attack on Hitler's elite in Mouen.

Return to the village and turn left on to the **D89A**. It can be appreciated that the narrow roads, hedgerows and small fields were not ideal terrain for the powerful Tigers of 101 Panzer *Schwere* Battalion which were being used more as static pill-boxes rather than tanks. They fell prey to determined infantrymen who had, unexpectedly, attacked from the flank. 4 SLI advanced through the Worcesters to clear this area.

On reaching the main Caen – Villers-Bocage road **(D675C)**, **turn right**. At the time of the battle this road was lightly built up along its length but today the ribbon development is much denser than it was in 1944. In Tourville, turn left onto the **D89** towards **Tourmauville** and **Esquay**. On the right is 15th Scottish Division's memorial ⓬ sited to overlook the objective of the Division's first battle, the River Odon.

Continue on down into the Odon Valley. This is the route taken by 2 A&SH to the **Tourmauville Bridge ⓭**, which they seized intact on the afternoon of 27 June. The Argyles formed a tight bridgehead with three companies south of the river with one to the north but were joined by 23 Hussars after half an hour, amidst much cheering.

Follow the road up, out of the Odon Valley. Turn left on the **D214** towards **Baron**. Drive through the village of Baron turn right at the statue of the Virgin and Child. Driving past a few houses the visitor breaks out into open country. Astride this Roman Road, 4 Armoured Brigade advanced up to **Hill 112** on the morning of 28 June. Park by the monuments at the cross roads ⓮ The monuments at the Croix des Filandriers commemorate the battle fought here by 43rd Wessex Division, supported by 31 Tank Brigade during Operation JUPITER on 10 July 1944. However, 4 Armoured Brigade suffered heavy casualties in both armour and men during 28 and 29 June, before tragically relinquishing Hill 112 to the Germans. The area was left littered with burnt out hulks of Shermans and M3 half-tracks.

From the memorials at the Croix des Filandriers

15th Scottish Division's Memorial on the road between Tourville and the Tourmauville Bridge

St Manvieu CWGC cemetery contains both British and German graves.

head west to le Bon Repos. Turn right after the garage onto the **D89**. To the left is the area where 44 RTR and 7 *Kompanie* 10 SS Pz Regt fought their encounter battle on 29 June  Turn left onto the **D214** towards **Gavrus**. Park by the church, which contains two British graves  One is unknown and the other belongs to a Gunner Lance Sergeant Donckley who was killed in action in the village on 29 June supporting 2 A&SH. Continue through Place Royal Welch Fusiliers (who reoccupied the village in July 1944) to the main **D139**. Turn right and drive down into the Odon Valley and the **double bridge**  held by the Argyles for three days against the overwhelmingly powerful counter-attacks of 10th *Frundsberg* SS Panzer Division.

Continue on the **D139**, up out of the Odon Valley towards **Grainville**. This is the area where 46 (Highland) Brigade fought the *Hohenstaufen* during II SS *Panzerkorps'* counter attack  Cross the **N175** and drive through Grainville. At the roundabout, turn left onto **the Rue de Carrouges** and, after several hundred yards, right onto the **Rue des Trois Buttes**. Looking down the drive by the white fencing, the visitor can see Chateau Grainville  the scene of the fighting on 29 June between the Royal Scots and 19 SS Pz Grs. **That concludes the EPSOM tour**.

Return to the roundabout. Turn left towards Tilly-sur-Seulles to return to Bayeux or right towards the N175 to return to the Caen area.

Appendix A
Order of Battle-OPERATION EPSOM
(PHASE ONE GROUPINGS)

VIII CORPS

11th ARMOURED DIVISION

HQ 11th ARMOURED DIVISION
11th Armoured Divisional Signal Regiment (-)

29th ARMOURED BRIGADE
23nd Hussars
3rd Battalion Royal Tank Regiment
2nd Fife and Forfar Yeomanry
8th Battalion, The Rifle Brigade
13th (HAC) Regiment Royal Horse Artillery
119th Battery, 75th Anti-Tank Regiment RA
Troop 612 Field Squadron
18 Light Field Ambulance RAMC
29th Brigade Workshop REME

159th INFANTRY BRIGADE
4th Battalion, Kings Shropshire Light Infantry
3rd Battalion Monmouthshire Regiment
1st Battalion Herefordshire Regiment
151st (Ayrshire Yeomanry) Field Regiment RA
117th Anti-tank Battery Royal Artillery
81 Squadron, 6 Assault Regiment Royal Engineers
(two Scissor Bridges)
2nd (Independent) Machine Gun Company Royal
Northumberland Fusiliers
Field Ambulance RAMC
159th Infantry Brigade Workshop REME
159th Infantry Brigade Company RASC

4th ARMOURED BRIGADE (under command for EPSOM)
The Royal Scots Greys
3rd County of London Yeomanry (The Sharpshooters)
44th Battalion, The Royal Tank Regiment
2nd Battalion, The King's Royal Rifle Corps
4th Regiment Royal Horse Artillery
144th (Self Propelled) Anti-Tank Battery RA
Field Ambulance RAMC
4th Armoured Brigade Workshop REME
4th Armoured Brigade Company RASC

11th ARMOURED DIVISIONAL TROOPS
2nd Northamptonshire Yeomanry
(less A Squadron) - Reconnaissance Regiment
270th Forward Delivery Squadron RAC
77th Medium Regiment Royal Artillery
(detached from 8 AGRA)
75th Anti-Tank Regiment RA (-)
58th Light Anti-Aircraft Regiment RA
(less two batteries)
Counter Mortar Battery RA
13 Field Squadron, 612th Field Squadron RE and
147th Field Park Squadron RE, 10th Bridging Troop

RE, Divisional Postal Unit RE
Field Dressing Station RAMC, Field Hygiene
Section RAMC
11th Armoured Divisional Troops Workshop REME
Ordnance Field Park Squadron RAOC
Divisional Troops RASC, Divisional Transport
Company RASC
11th Armoured Division Provost Company RCMP

15th SCOTTISH DIVISION

HQ 15th SCOTTISH INFANTRY DIVISION
15 Scottish Divisional Signals Regiment (-)

31st TANK BRIGADE (under command for EPSOM)
31st Tank Brigade Signal Squadron
7th Battalion, The Royal Tank Regiment
B Squadron, 22nd Dragoons (Flails)
9th Battalion, The Royal Tank Regiment
C Squadron, The Westminster Dragoons (Flails)
31st Tank Brigade Workshop REME

44th LOWLAND INFANTRY BRIGADE
8th Battalion, The Royal Scots
6th Battalion, The Kings Own Scottish Border
Regiment
6th Battalion, The Royal Scots Fusiliers
141st (The Buffs) Regiment RAC (two troops Crocodile)
190th Field Regiment Regimental Artillery
159th Anti-Tank Battery Royal Artillery
81st Squadron, 6 Assault Regiment Royal Engineers
(two troops AVRE)
279th Field Company Royal Engineers
A (Machine gun) Company 1st Middlesex Regiment
(including a Heavy Mortar Platoon)
193rd Field Ambulance
Light Anti-Aircraft Battery
2nd Company Divisional Signal Regiment
283rd Company Royal Army Service Corps

46th HIGHLAND INFANTRY BRIGADE
2nd Battalion, The Glasgow Highlanders
7th Battalion, The Seaforth Highlanders
9th Battalion, The Cameronian Highlanders
A Squadron, 2nd Northamptonshire Yeomanry
(under command for movement)
141st (The Buffs) Regiment RAC
(two troops Crocodiles)
181st Field Regiment Royal Artillery
161st Anti-Tank Battery Royal Artillery
81 Squadron, 6 Assault Regiment Royal Engineers
(three troops AVRE)
278th Field Company Royal Engineers
B (Machine gun) Company 1st Middlesex Regiment
(including a Heavy Mortar Platoon)
194th Field Ambulance

Light Anti-Aircraft Battery
3rd Company 15th Divisional Signals Regiment
284th Company Royal Army Service Corps

227th HIGHLAND INFANTRY BRIGADE
10th Battalion The Highland Light Infantry
2nd Battalion The Argyll & Sutherland Highlanders
2nd Battalion The Gordon Highlanders
131st Field Regiment Royal Artillery
286th Anti-Tank Battery Royal Artillery
20th Field Company Royal Engineers
C (Machinegun) Company 1st Middlesex Regiment
(including a Heavy Mortar Platoon)
153rd Field Ambulance
391st Light Anti-Aircraft Battery Royal Artillery
4th Company 15th Divisional Signal Regiment
62nd Company Royal Army Service Corps

15th SCOTTISH DIVISIONAL TROOPS
15th Reconnaissance Regiment RAC
HQ 97th Anti-Tank Regiment Royal Artillery and 346th Battery
HQ 119th Light Anti-Aircraft Regiment RA
HQ 15th Division Engineers Regiment, 624th Field Park Company and 15th Divisional Postal Unit
26th Bridging Platoon RE
HQ 1st (Machine gun) Battalion, The Middlesex Regiment
Royal Army Service Corps HQ 15th Division RAOC Battalion and 399th Company RASC
Royal Army Medical Corps 22nd Field Dressing Section and 49th Field Hygiene Section
Royal Army Ordnance Corps 15th Ordnance Field Park and 305th Mobile Laundry & Bath Unit
Royal Electrical and Mechanical Engineers 44th Infantry Brigade Workshop, 46th Infantry Brigade Workshop 227th Infantry Brigade Workshop and 15th Infantry Troops Workshop
Military Police 15th Division Company Royal Corps of Military Police
Field Security Section 39th Section Intelligence Corps

43rd WESSEX INFANTRY DIVISION

HQ 43rd (WESSEX) INFANTRY DIVISION
43rd (Wessex) Divisional Signals Regiment (-)

HQ 129th INFANTRY BRIGADE
4th Battalion, The Somerset Light Infantry
4th Battalion, The Wiltshire Regiment
5th Battalion, The Wiltshire Regiment
94th (Dorset and Hampshire) Field Regiment Royal Artillery
235th Anti-Tank Battery
206th Field Company Royal Engineers
A (Machine gun) Company 8th Middlesex
(including a Heavy Mortar Platoon)
129th Field Ambulance
Support Troop 360th Light Anti-Aircraft Battery
30th Independent Anti-Aircraft Troop
2nd Company Divisional Signal Regiment

504th Company Royal Army Service Corps

HQ 130th INFANTRY BRIGADE
7th Battalion, The Hampshire Regiment
4th Battalion, The Dorsetshire Regiment
5th Battalion, The Dorsetshire Regiment
112th (Wessex) Field Regiment Royal Artillery
223rd Anti-Tank Battery
553rd Field Company Royal Engineers
B (Machine gun) Company 8th Middlesex
(including a Heavy Mortar Platoon)
130th Field Ambulance
Support Troop 362th Light Anti-Aircraft Battery
32nd Independent Anti-Aircraft Troop
3rd Company 43rd Divisional Signals Regiment
505th Company Royal Army Service Corps

HQ 214th INFANTRY BRIGADE
7th Battalion Somerset Light Infantry
1st Battalion The Worcestershire Regiment
5th Battalion Duke of Cornwall's Light Infantry
179th Field Regiment Royal Artillery
333rd Anti-Tank Battery Royal Artillery
204th Field Company Royal Engineers
C (Machine gun) Company 8th Middlesex
(including a Heavy Mortar Platoon)
213th Field Ambulance
Support Troop 361st Light Anti-Aircraft Battery
31st Independent Anti-Aircraft Troop
4th Company 43rd Divisional Signal Regiment
45th Company Royal Army Service Corps

43rd WESSEX DIVISIONAL TROOPS
43rd (Gloucester) Reconnaissance Regiment (Not in action during EPSOM)
HQ 59th Anti-Tank Regiment Royal Artillery (Hampshire DoC) and 236th Battery
HQ 110th Light Anti-Aircraft Regiment RA (7th Dorsets), 360th Battery (-) and 362nd Battery (-)
HQ 43rd Division Engineers Regiment, 207th Field Park Company and 43rd Divisional Postal Unit
HQ 8th (Machine gun) Battalion, The Middlesex Regiment
Royal Army Service Corps HQ 43rd Divisional RAOC Battalion and 506th Company RAOC
Royal Army Medical Corps 14th Field Dressing Section, 15th Field Dressing Section and 38th Field Hygiene Section
Royal Army Ordnance Corps 43rd Division Ordnance Field Park and 306th Mobile Bath Unit
Royal Electrical and Mechanical Engineers 129th Infantry Brigade Workshop, 130th Infantry Brigade Workshop and 214th Infantry Brigade Workshop
Military Police 43rd Division Company Royal Corps of Military Police
Intelligence Corps 57th Field Security Section

VII CORPS TROOPS
91st Anti-Tank Regiment Royal Artillery
121st Anti-Aircraft Regiment Royal Artillery

21st ARMY GROUP TROOPS (under Command VIII

Corps for EPSOM)
    8th Army Group Royal Artillery

79th ARMOURED DIVISION TROOPS
    141st Regimental RAC (Crocodiles)

XXX CORPS

49th (WEST RIDING) INFANTRY DIVISION

HQ 49th (WEST RIDING) INFANTRY DIVISION
    49th (West Riding) Divisional Signals Regiement (-)

HQ 70th INFANTRY BRIGADE
    1st Battalion, The Tyneside Scottish
    10th Battalion, The Durham Light Infantry
    11th Battalion, The Durham Light Infantry
    185th Field Regiment Royal Artillery
    217th Anti-Tank Battery
    757th Field Company Royal Engineers
    C (Machine gun) Company 2nd Kensington
    (including a Heavy Mortar Platoon)
    187th Field Ambulance RAMC
    Support Troop, Light Anti-Aircraft Battery
    3rd Company Divisional Signal Regiment
    482nd Company Royal Army Service Corps
    70th Infantry Brigade Workshop REME

HQ 146th INFANTRY BRIGADE
    1/4th Battalion, The Lincolnshire Regiment
    4th Battalion, The King's Own Yorkshire Light
    Infantry
    Hallamshire Battalion, The Yorkshire & Lancashire
    Regiment
    69th Field Regiment Royal Artillery
    218th Anti-Tank Battery
    294th Field Company Royal Engineers
    A (Machine gun) Company 2nd Kensington
    (including a Heavy Mortar Platoon)
    146th Field Ambulance
    Support Troop, Light Anti-Aircraft Battery
    1st Company 43rd Divisional Signals Regiment
    460th Company Royal Army Service Corps
    146th Infantry Brigade Workshop REME

HQ 147th INFANTRY BRIGADE
    11th Battalion The Royal Scots
    6th Battalion The Duke of Wellington's Regiment
    7th Battalion The Duke of Wellington's Regiment
    143th Field Regiment Royal Artillery
    219th Anti-Tank Battery Royal Artillery
    756th Field Company Royal Engineers
    B (Machine gun) Company 2nd Kensington
    (including a Heavy Mortar Platoon)
    160th Field Ambulance
    Support Troop, Light Anti-Aircraft Battery
    4th Company 43rd Divisional Signal Regiment
    483rd Company Royal Army Service Corps
    147th Infantry Brigade Workshop REME

49th (WEST RIDING) DIVISIONAL TROOPS
    49th Reconnaissance Regiment
    HQ 55th Anti-Tank Regiment Artillery (Suffolk
    Yeomanry) and 220th Battery
    HQ 89th Light Anti-Aircraft Regiment RA
    HQ 49th Division Engineers Regiment 289th Field
    Park Company and 49th Divisional Postal Unit
    HQ 2nd (Machine gun) Battalion, The Kensington
    Regiment
    Royal Army Service Corps HQ 49th Division
    RAOC Battalion and 118th Company RAOC
    Royal Army Medical Corps 16th Field Dressing
    Section, 17th Field Dressing Section and 35th Field
    Hygiene Section
    Royal Army Ordnance Corps 49th Division
    Ordnance Field Park, 149 Ordnance Sub Park and
    308th Mobile Bath Unit
    Royal Electrical and Mechanical Engineers HQ
    REME and 49th Div Troops Workshop
    Military Police 49th Division Company Royal
    Corps of Military Police
    Intelligence Corps 60th Field Security Section

8th ARMOURED BRIGADE
    24th Lancers
    4th/7th Dragoon Guards
    1 Notts Yeomanry
    12th Battalion Kings Royal Rifle Corps
    147th Essex Yeomanry Field Regiment (Self
    Propelled) Anti-Tank Battery Royal Artillery
    8th Armoured Brigade Signal Squadron

ARTILLERY ALLOCATED TO EPSOM

11 Armoured Division - 48 x 25 Pounder (field guns)
   15 (Scottish) Division - 96 x 25 Pounder guns
   43 (Wessex) Division - 72 x 25 Pounder guns
   4 Armoured Brigade - 24 x 25 Pounder guns
   8th Army Group RA - 16 x heavy guns
            16 x 5.5 & 4.5 (medium) guns
            24 x 4.7" (Heavy) anti-aircraft guns
            (296 guns)
   Available from flanking corps.
   I Corps - 216 field guns
           32 medium guns
           16 heavy guns
   XXX Corps - 96 field guns
           64 medium guns
           16 heavy guns
           (440)
Total   736

APPENDIX B

Advice to Visitors

Preparation and planning are important prerequisites for an enjoyable and successful tour. This section aims to give some advice to those who are travelling to Normandy for the first time and acts as a checklist for the more seasoned traveller.

Travel to Normandy

Most visitors travelling to the Normandy battlefields do so by car. However, with the area's proximity to ports, an increasing number of visitors are cycling around the battlefields. However one travels around Normandy, a journey originating in the UK has to cross the Channel. A wide range of options available available. The nearest ferry service to the Caen area is the Brittany Ferries route, which takes the visitor from Portsmouth to Ousitreham, less than half an hour's drive from the EPSOM area. This crossing is slightly longer than others, being six hours during the day or six hours thirty minutes overnight. Further away, just over an hour to the west, is the port of Cherbourg, which is served by sailings from Portsmouth, and Poole (four hours thirty minutes to five hours). Two hours drive to the east is le Harve, which is served by ferries from Portsmouth. Choice for most visitors depends on the convenience of the sailing times and, of course, relative costs. To the east of Normandy are the shorter, and consequently cheaper, crossings in the Boulogne and Calais area. For those who dislike ferries there is the Channel Tunnel, but this option, though quicker, can be more expensive. Internet deals can be attractive. From the Calais area, EPSOM country can be easily reached via the new autoroutes in just over four hours but bear in mind tolls cost up to £15. This can be reduced by about £5 by avoiding the new Pont de Normandie. It is worth checking out all the options available and make your selection of routes based on UK travel, ferry times and cost. French law requires you to carry a full driving licence and a vehicle registration document. Do not forget your passport and a GB sticker if you do not have EU number plates with the blue national identifier square.

Insurance

It is important to check that you are properly insured to travel to France. Firstly, consult your insurance broker to ensure that you are covered for driving outside the UK and, secondly, make sure you have health cover. Form E111, available from main post offices, grants the bearer reciprocal treatment rights in France but, even so, the visitor may wish to consider a comprehensive package of travel insurance. Such packages are available from a broker or travel agent. It is a legal requirement for a driver to carry a valid certificate of motor insurance. Be warned that without insurance, repatriating the sick or injured is very expensive, as is return of vehicles.

Accommodation

There are no hotels in the immediate EPSOM area. However, in Caen there is a wide variety of accommadition ranging from five star to chambres d'hotel. Up to date contact details are available from the French Tourist Office, 178 Picadilly, London W1V 0AL (01891 244 123). Further details of accommodation and travel amenities are available from the office of Calvados Tourisme, Place du Canada, 14000 Caen, France. To telephone from the UK dial 0033, drop the 0 necessary for ringing with France and dial 2 31 86 53 30.

Maps

Good maps are an essential prerequisite to a successful battlefield visit. Best of all is a combination of contemporary and modern maps. The Battleground series of course, provides a variety of maps. However, a number of modern map series are available in both the UK and Normandy. Most readily available in both countries are the Michelin 1:200,000 Yellow Series. Sheet 54 covers the British and US D Day build-up and break-out battle areas and is useful for getting around the Normandy battlefield and its ports. Better still are the Institut Geographique National (IGN) 1:100,000 Serie Vert (Green Series) maps. Sheet 6, Caen-Cherbourg-Normandie, covers most of the Normandy battle area. Normally only available in the UK at a specialist map shop, they can, however, be procured as a special order through high street book shops such as Waterstones. The Series Vert maps have the advantage of showing contours and other details such as unmade roads and tracks. Sheet 6 is a good compromise if you are visiting several sites and wish to use a single map. The most detailed maps, readily available in France, are the IGN Serie Bleue in 1:25,000 scale. The EPSOM area is covered by the sheets: 1512 O Bayeux, 1513 O Villers-Bocage, 1513 E Evrecy, which together cover Norrey-en-Bessin, Cheux, the Odon Valley and Hill 112. This map can normally be found in the tourist shops at Arromanches. However, if you are planning your tour well in advance, large retailers in the UK can order Serie Bleue maps, given sufficient notice. The London map retailer Stamfords, provides a quick and easy method of ordering IGN maps over the internet.

Courtesy

Much of the EPSOM battle area is open farmland but many of the villages in the area became German strong points and therefore, form a part of the battlefield. Please respect private property in both open country and villages, particularly avoiding driving on unmade up farm tracks and entering non-public areas in villages. Adequate views of the scene of the action can be enjoyed from public land and rights of way. In all cases, please be careful not to block roads by careless car parking. The people of Normandy extend a genuine welcome to those who come to honour the memory of their liberators. To preserve this welcome please respect the local people and their property.

APPENDIX C

SS Ranks and their British and US equivalents

Waffen SS		British Army	US Army
SS-*Brigadeführer*		Brigadier	Brigadier General
SS-*Oberführer*		(not applicable)	Senior Colonel
SS-*Standartenführer*		Colonel	Colonel
SS-*Obersturmbannführer*		Lieutenant Colonel	Lieutenant Colonel
SS-*Sturmbannführer*		Major	Major
SS-*Hauptsturmführer*		Captain	Captain
SS-*Obersturmführer*		Lieutenant	1st Lieutenant
SS-*Untersturmführer*		2nd Lieutenant	2nd Lieutenant
SS-*Sturmscharführer*		Regimental Sergeant Major	Sergeant Major
SS-*Hauptscharführer*		Sergeant Major	Master Sergeant
SS-*Oberscharführer*		(not applicable)	Technical Sergeant
SS-*Scharführer*		Colour Sergeant	Staff Sergeant
SS-*Unterscharführer*		Sergeant	Sergeant
SS-*Rottenführer*		Corporal	Corporal
SS-*Sturmmann*		Lance Corporal	(not applicable)
SS-*Oberschütze*		(not applicable)	Private 1st Class
SS-*Mann*		Private	Private

INDEX